A Soul's Tragedy & Luria by Robert Browning

Bells and Pomegranates Number VIII

Robert Browning is one of the most significant Victorian Poets and, of course, English Poetry.

Much of his reputation is based upon his mastery of the dramatic monologue although his talents encompassed verse plays and even a well-regarded essay on Shelley during a long and prolific career.

He was born on May 7th, 1812 in Walmouth, London. Much of his education was home based and Browning was an eclectic and studious student, learning several languages and much else across a myriad of subjects, interests and passions.

Browning's early career began promisingly. The fragment from his intended long poem Pauline brought him to the attention of Dante Gabriel Rossetti, and was followed by Paracelsus, which was praised by both William Wordsworth and Charles Dickens. In 1840 the difficult Sordello, which was seen as willfully obscure, brought his career almost to a standstill.

Despite these artistic and professional difficulties his personal life was about to become immensely fulfilling. He began a relationship with, and then married, the older and better known Elizabeth Barrett. This new foundation served to energise his writings, his life and his career.

During their time in Italy they both wrote much of their best work. With her untimely death in 1861 he returned to London and thereafter began several further major projects.

The collection Dramatis Personae (1864) and the book-length epic poem The Ring and the Book (1868-69) were published and well received; his reputation as a venerated English poet now assured.

Robert Browning died in Venice on December 12th, 1889.

Index of Contents

A SOUL'S TRAGEDY

ACT FIRST, BEING WHAT WAS CALLED THE POETRY OF CHIAPPINO'S LIFE; AND ACT SECOND, ITS PROSE

PERSONS
LUITOLFO and EULALIA, betrothed lovers.
CHIAPPINO, their friend.
OGNIBEN, the Pope's Legate.
Citizens of Faenza.

TIME: 15—.

PLACE: Faenza

ACT I

Inside Luitolfo's house.

CHIAPPINO, EULALIA.

EULALIA
What is it keeps Luitolfo? Night 's fast falling,
And 't was scarce sunset ... had the ave-bell
Sounded before he sought the Provost's house?
I think not: all he had to say would take
Few minutes, such a very few, to say!
How do you think, Chiappino? If our lord
The Provost were less friendly to your friend
Than everybody here professes him,
I should begin to tremble—should not you?
Why are you silent when so many times
I turn and speak to you?

CHIAPPINO
That 's good!

EULALIA
You laugh!

CHIAPPINO
Yes. I had fancied nothing that bears price
In the whole world was left to call my own;
And, maybe, felt a little pride thereat.
Up to a single man's or woman's love,
Down to the right in my own flesh and blood,
There 's nothing mine, I fancied,—till you spoke:
—Counting, you see, as "nothing" the permission
To study this peculiar lot of mine
In silence: well, go silence with the rest
Of the world's good! What can I say, shall serve?

EULALIA
This,—lest you, even more than needs, embitter
Our parting: say your wrongs have cast, for once,
A cloud across your spirit!

CHIAPPINO
How a cloud?

EULALIA
No man nor woman loves you, did you say?

CHIAPPINO
My God, were 't not for thee!

EULALIA
Ay, God remains,
Even did men forsake you.

CHIAPPINO
Oh, not so!
Were 't not for God, I mean, what hope of truth—
Speaking truth, hearing truth, would stay with man?
I, now—the homeless friendless penniless
Proscribed and exiled wretch who speak to you,—
Ought to speak truth, yet could not, for my death,
(The thing that tempts me most) help speaking lies
About your friendship and Luitolfo's courage
And all our townsfolk's equanimity—
Through sheer incompetence to rid myself
Of the old miserable lying trick
Caught from the liars I have lived with,—God,
Did I not turn to thee! It is thy prompting

I dare to be ashamed of, and thy counsel
Would die along my coward lip, I know.
But I do turn to thee. This craven tongue,
These features which refuse the soul its way,
Reclaim thou! Give me truth—truth, power to speak
—And after be sole present to approve
The spoken truth! Or, stay, that spoken truth,
Who knows but you, too, may approve?

EULALIA
Ah, well—
Keep silence then, Chiappino!

CHIAPPINO
You would hear,—
You shall now,—why the thing we please to style
My gratitude to you and all your friends
For service done me, is just gratitude
So much as yours was service: no whit more.
I was born here, so was Luitolfo; both
At one time, much with the same circumstance
Of rank and wealth; and both, up to this night
Of parting company, have side by side
Still fared, he in the sunshine—I, the shadow.
"Why?" asks the world. "Because," replies the world
To its complacent self, "these playfellows,
Who took at church the holy-water drop
Each from the other's finger, and so forth,—
Were of two moods: Luitolfo was the proper
Friend-making, everywhere friend-finding soul,
Fit for the sunshine, so, it followed him.
A happy-tempered bringer of the best
Out of the worst; who bears with what 's past cure,
And puts so good a face on 't—wisely passive
Where action 's fruitless, while he remedies
In silence what the foolish rail against;
A man to smooth such natures as parade
Of opposition must exasperate;
No general gauntlet-gatherer for the weak
Against the strong, yet over-scrupulous
At lucky junctures; one who won't forego
The after-battle work of binding wounds,
Because, forsooth he 'd have to bring himself
To side with wound-inflictors for their leave!"
—Why do you gaze, nor help me to repeat
What comes so glibly from the common mouth,
About Luitolfo and his so-styled friend?

EULALIA
Because, that friend's sense is obscured ...

CHIAPPINO
I thought
You would be readier with the other half
Of the world's story, my half! Yet, 't is true.
For all the world does say it. Say your worst!
True, I thank God, I ever said "you sin,"
When a man did sin: if I could not say it,
I glared it at him; if I could not glare it,
I prayed against him; then my part seemed over.
God's may begin yet: so it will, I trust.

EULALIA
If the world outraged you, did we?

CHIAPPINO
What 's "me"
That you use well or ill? It 's man, in me,
All your successes are an outrage to,
You all, whom sunshine follows, as you say!
Here 's our Faenza birthplace; they send here
A provost from Ravenna: how he rules,
You can at times be eloquent about.
"Then, end his rule!"—" Ah yes, one stroke does that!
But patience under wrong works slow and sure.
Must violence still bring peace forth? He, beside,
Returns so blandly one's obeisance! ah—
Some latent virtue may be lingering yet,
Some human sympathy which, once excite,
And all the lump were leavened quietly:
So, no more talk of striking, for this time!"
But I, as one of those he rules, won't bear
These pretty takings-up and layings-down
Our cause, just as you think occasion suits.
Enough of earnest, is there? You'll play, will you?
Diversify your tactics, give submission,
Obsequiousness and flattery a turn,
While we die in our misery patient deaths?
We all are outraged then, and I the first:
I, for mankind, resent each shrug and smirk,
Each beck and bend, each ... all you do and are,
I hate!

EULALIA
We share a common censure, then.
'T is well you have not poor Luitolfo's part

Nor mine to point out in the wide offence.

CHIAPPINO
Oh, shall I let you so escape me, lady?
Come, on your own ground, lady,—from yourself,
(Leaving the people's wrong, which most is mine)
What have I got to be so grateful for?
These three last fines, no doubt, one on the other
Paid by Luitolfo?

EULALIA
Shame, Chiappino!

CHIAPPINO
Shame
Fall presently on who deserves it most!
—Which is to see. He paid my fines—my friend,
Your prosperous smooth lover presently,
Then, scarce your wooer,—soon, your husband: well—
I loved you.

EULALIA
Hold!

CHIAPPINO
You knew it, years ago.
When my voice faltered and my eye grew dim
Because you gave me your silk mask to hold—
My voice that greatens when there 's need to curse
The people's Provost to their heart's content,
—My eye, the Provost, who bears all men's eyes,
Banishes now because he cannot bear,—
You knew ... but you do your parts—my part, I:
So be it! You flourish, I decay: all 's well.

EULALIA
I hear this for the first time.

CHIAPPINO
The fault 's there?
Then my days spoke not, and my nights of fire
Were voiceless? Then the very heart may burst.
Yet all prove naught, because no mincing speech
Tells leisurely that thus it is and thus?
Eulalia, truce with toying for this once!
A banished fool, who troubles you to-night
For the last time—why, what 's to fear from me?
You knew I loved you!

EULALIA

Not so, on my faith!
You were my now-affianced lover's friend—
Came in, went out with him, could speak as he.
All praise your ready parts and pregnant wit;
See how your words come from you in a crowd!
Luitolfo 's first to place you o'er himself
In all that challenges respect and love:
Yet you were silent then, who blame me now.
I say all this by fascination, sure:
I, all but wed to one I love, yet listen!
It must be, you are wronged, and that the wrongs
Luitolfo pities ...

CHIAPPINO

—You too pity? Do!
But hear first what my wrongs are; so began
This talk and so shall end this talk. I say,
Was 't not enough that I must strive (I saw)
To grow so far familiar with your charms
As next contrive some way to win them—which
To do, an age seemed far too brief—for, see!
We all aspire to heaven; and there lies heaven
Above us: go there! Dare we go? no, surely!
How dare we go without a reverent pause,
A growing less unfit for heaven? Just so,
I dared not speak: the greater fool, it seems!
Was 't not enough to struggle with such folly,
But I must have, beside, the very man
Whose slight free loose and incapacious soul
Gave his tongue scope to say whate'er he would
—Must have him load me with his benefits
—For fortune's fiercest stroke?

EULALIA

Justice to him
That 's now entreating, at his risk perhaps,
Justice for you! Did he once call those acts
Of simple friendship—bounties, benefits?

CHIAPPINO

No: the straight course had been to call them thus.
Then, I had flung them back, and kept myself
Unhampered, free as he to win the prize
We both sought. But "the gold was dross," he said:
"He loved me, and I loved him not: why spurn
A trifle out of superfluity?

He had forgotten he had done as much."
So had not I! Henceforth, try as I could
To take him at his word, there stood by you
My benefactor; who might speak and laugh
And urge his nothings, even banter me
Before you—but my tongue was tied. A dream!
Let 's wake: your husband ... how you shake at that!
Good—my revenge!

EULALIA
Why should I shake? What forced
Or forces me to be Luitolfo's bride?

CHIAPPINO
There 's my revenge, that nothing forces you.
No gratitude, no liking of the eye
Nor longing of the heart, but the poor bond
Of habit—here so many times he came,
So much he spoke,—all these compose the tie
That pulls you from me. Well, he paid my fines,
Nor missed, a cloak from wardrobe, dish from table;
He spoke a good word to the Provost here,
Held me up when my fortunes fell away,
—It had not looked so well to let me drop,—
Men take pains to preserve a tree-stump, even,
Whose boughs they played beneath—much more a friend.
But one grows tired of seeing, after the first,
Pains spent upon impracticable stuff
Like me. I could not change: you know the rest:
I 've spoke my mind too fully out, by chance,
This morning to our Provost; so, ere night
I leave the city on pain of death. And now
On my account there 's gallant intercession
Goes forward—that 's so graceful!—and anon
He 'll noisily come back: "the intercession
Was made and fails; all 's over for us both;
'T is vain contending; I would better go."
And I do go—and straight to you he turns
Light of a load; and ease of that permits
His visage to repair the natural bland
Œconomy, sore broken late to suit
My discontent. Thus, all are pleased—you, with him,
He with himself, and all of you with me
—"Who," say the citizens, "had done far better
In letting people sleep upon their woes,
If not possessed with talent to relieve them
When once awake;—but then I had," they 'll say,
"Doubtless some unknown compensating pride

In what I did; and as I seem content
With ruining myself, why, so should they be."
And so they are, and so be with his prize
The devil, when he gets them speedily!
Why does not your Luitolfo come? I long
To don this cloak and take the Lugo path.
It seems you never loved me, then?

EULALIA
Chiappino!

CHIAPPINO
Never?

EULALIA
Never.

CHIAPPINO
That 's sad. Say what I might,
There was no help from being sure this while
You loved me. Love like mine must have return,
I thought: no river starts but to some sea.
And had you loved me, I could soon devise
Some specious reason why you stifled love,
Some fancied self-denial on your part,
Which made you choose Luitolfo; so, excepting
From the wide condemnation of all here,
One woman. Well, the other dream may break!
If I knew any heart, as mine loved you,
Loved me, though in the vilest breast 't were lodged,
I should, I think, be forced to love again:
Else there 's no right nor reason in the world.

EULALIA
"If you knew," say you,—but I did not know.
That 's where you 're blind, Chiappino!—a disease
Which if I may remove, I 'll not repent
The listening to. You cannot, will not, see
How, place you but in every circumstance
Of us, you are just now indignant at,
You 'd be as we.

CHIAPPINO
I should be?... that; again!
I, to my friend, my country and my love,
Be as Luitolfo and these Faentines?

EULALIA

As we.

CHIAPPINO
Now, I 'll say something to remember.
I trust in nature for the stable laws
Of beauty and utility.—Spring shall plant,
And Autumn garner to the end of time:
I trust in God—the right shall be the right
And other than the wrong, while he endures:
I trust in my own soul, that can perceive
The outward and the inward, nature's good
And God's: so, seeing these men and myself,
Having a right to speak, thus do I speak.
I 'll not curse—God bears with them, well may I—
But I—protest against their claiming me.
I simply say, if that 's allowable,
I would not (broadly) do as they have done.
—God curse this townful of born slaves, bred slaves,
Branded into the blood and bone, slaves! Curse
Whoever loves, above his liberty,
House, land or life! and ...

[A knocking without.

—bless my hero-friend,
Luitolfo!

EULALIA
How he knocks!

CHIAPPINO
The peril, lady!
"Chiappino, I have run a risk—a risk!
For when I prayed the Provost (he 's my friend)
To grant you a week's respite of the sentence
That confiscates your goods, exiles yourself,
He shrugged his shoulder—I say, shrugged it! Yes,
And fright of that drove all else from my head.
Here 's a good purse of scudi: off with you,
Lest of that shrug come what God only knows!
The scudi—friend, they 're trash—no thanks, I beg!
Take the north gate,—for San Vitale's suburb,
Whose double taxes you appealed against,
In discomposure at your ill-success
Is apt to stone you: there, there—only go!
Beside, Eulalia here looks sleepily.
Shake ... oh, you hurt me, so you squeeze my wrist!"
—Is it not thus you 'll speak, adventurous friend?

[As he opens the door, **LUITOLFO** rushes in, his garments disordered.

EULALIA
Luitolfo! Blood?

LUITOLFO
There 's more—and more of it!
Eulalia—take the garment! No—you, friend!
You take it and the blood from me—you dare!

EULALIA
Oh, who has hurt you? where's the wound?

CHIAPPINO
"Who," say you?
The man with many a touch of virtue yet!
The Provost's friend has proved too frank of speech,
And this comes of it. Miserable hound!
This comes of temporizing, as I said!
Here 's fruit of your smooth speeches and soft looks!
Now see my way! As God lives, I go straight
To the palace and do justice, once for all!

LUITOLFO
What says he?

CHIAPPINO
I'll do justice on him.

LUITOLFO
Him?

CHIAPPINO
The Provost.

LUITOLFO
I 've just killed him.

EULALIA
Oh, my God!

LUITOLFO
My friend, they 're on my trace; they 'll have me—now!
They 're round him, busy with him: soon they 'll find
He 's past their help, and then they 'll be on me!
Chiappino, save Eulalia! I forget ...
Were you not bound for ...

CHIAPPINO
Lugo?

LUITOLFO
Ah—yes—yes!
That was the point I prayed of him to change.
Well, go—be happy! Is Eulalia safe?
They 're on me!

CHIAPPINO
'T is through me they reach you, then!
Friend, seem the man you are! Lock arms—that 's right!
Now tell me what you 've done; explain how you,
That still professed forbearance, still preached peace,
Could bring yourself ...

LUITOLFO
What was peace for, Chiappino?
I tried peace: did that promise, when peace failed,
Strife should not follow? All my peaceful days
Were just the prelude to a day like this.
I cried "You call me 'friend': save my true friend!
Save him, or lose me!"

CHIAPPINO
But you never said
You meant to tell the Provost thus and thus.

LUITOLFO
Why should I say it? What else did I mean?

CHIAPPINO
Well? He persisted?

LUITOLFO
—"Would so order it
You should not trouble him too soon again."
I saw a meaning in his eye and lip;
I poured my heart's store of indignant words
Out on him: then—I know not! He retorted.
And I ... some staff lay there to hand—I think
He bade his servants thrust me out—I struck ...
Ah, they come! Fly you, save yourselves, you two!
The dead back-weight of the beheading axe!
The glowing trip-hook, thumbscrews and the gadge!

EULALIA

They do come! Torches in the Place! Farewell,
Chiappino! You can work no good to us—
Much to yourself; believe not, all the world
Must needs be cursed henceforth!

CHIAPPINO
And you?

EULALIA
I stay.

CHIAPPINO
Ha, ha! Now, listen! I am master here!
This was my coarse disguise; this paper shows
My path of flight and place of refuge—see—
Lugo, Argenta, past San Nicolo,
Ferrara, then to Venice and all 's safe!
Put on the cloak! His people have to fetch
A compass round about. There 's time enough
Ere they can reach us, so you straightway make
For Lugo ... nay, he hears not! On with it—
The cloak, Luitolfo, do you hear me? See—
He obeys he knows not how. Then, if I must—
Answer me! Do you know the Lugo gate?

EULALIA
The northwest gate, over the bridge?

LUITOLFO
I know.

CHIAPPINO
Well, there—you are not frightened? all my route
Is traced in that: at Venice you escape
Their power. Eulalia, I am master here!

[Shouts from without. He pushes out **LUITOLFO**, who complies mechanically.

In time! Nay, help me with him—so! He 's gone.

EULALIA
What have you done? On you, perchance, all know
The Provost's hater, will men's vengeance fall
As our accomplice.

CHIAPPINO
Mere accomplice? See!

[Putting on **LUITOLFO'S** vest.

Now, lady, am I true to my profession,
Or one of these?

EULALIA
You take Luitolfo's place?

CHIAPPINO
Die for him.

EULALIA
Well done!

[Shouts increase.

CHIAPPINO
How the people tarry!
I can't be silent; I must speak: or sing—
How natural to sing now!

EULALIA
Hush and pray!
We are to die; but even I perceive
'T is not a very hard thing so to die.
My cousin of the pale-blue tearful eyes,
Poor Cesca, suffers more from one day's life
With the stern husband; Tisbe's heart goes forth
Each evening after that wild son of hers,
To track his thoughtless footstep through the streets:
How easy for them both to die like this!
I am not sure that I could live as they.

CHIAPPINO
Here they come, crowds! they pass the gate? Yes!—No!—
One torch is in the courtyard. Here flock all.

EULALIA
At least Luitolfo has escaped. What cries!

CHIAPPINO
If they would drag one to the marketplace,
One might speak there!

EULALIA
List, list!

CHIAPPINO

They mount the steps.

[Enter the **POPULACE**

CHIAPPINO
I killed the Provost!

THE POPULACE [Speaking together]
'T was Chiappino, friends!
Our savior! The best man at last as first!
He who first made us feel what chains we wore,
He also strikes the blow that shatters them,
He at last saves us—our best citizen!
—Oh, have you only courage to speak now?
My eldest son was christened a year since
"Cino" to keep Chiappino's name in mind—
Cino, for shortness merely, you observe!
The city 's in our hands. The guards are fled.
Do you, the cause of all, come down—come up—
Come out to counsel us, our chief, our king,
Whate'er rewards you! Choose your own reward!
The peril over, its reward begins!
Come and harangue us in the market-place!

EULALIA
Chiappino?

CHIAPPINO
Yes—I understand your eyes!
You think I should have promptlier disowned
This deed with its strange unforeseen success,
In favor of Luitolfo. But the peril,
So far from ended, hardly seems begun.
To-morrow, rather, when a calm succeeds,
We easily shall make him full amends:
And meantime—if we save them as they pray,
And justify the deed by its effects?

EULALIA
You would, for worlds, you had denied at once.

CHIAPPINO
I know my own intention, be assured!
All 's well. Precede us, fellow-citizens!

The Market-place. **LUITOLFO** in disguise mingling with the **POPULACE** assembled opposite the Provost's Palace.

1st BYSTANDER [To **LUITOLFO**]
You, a friend of Luitolfo's? Then, your friend is vanished,—in all probability killed on the night that his patron the tyrannical Provost was loyally suppressed here, exactly a month ago, by our illustrious fellow-citizen, thrice-noble savior, and new Provost that is like to be, this very morning,—Chiappino!

LUITOLFO
He the new Provost?

2nd BYSTANDER
Up those steps will he go, and beneath yonder pillar stand, while Ogniben, the Pope's Legate from Ravenna, reads the new dignitary's title to the people, according to established custom: for which reason, there is the assemblage you inquire about.

LUITOLFO
Chiappino—the late Provost's successor? Impossible! But tell me of that presently. What I would know first of all is, wherefore Luitolfo must so necessarily have been killed on that memorable night?

3rd BYSTANDER
You were Luitolfo's friend? So was I. Never, if you will credit me, did there exist so poor-spirited a milk-sop. He, with all the opportunities in the world, furnished by daily converse with our oppressor, would not stir a finger to help us: and, when Chiappino rose in solitary majesty and ... how does one go on saying?... dealt the godlike blow,—this Luitolfo, not unreasonably fearing the indignation of an aroused and liberated people, fled precipitately. He may have got trodden to death in the press at the southeast gate, when the Provost's guards fled through it to Ravenna, with their wounded master,—if he did not rather hang himself under some hedge.

LUITOLFO
Or why not simply have lain perdue in some quiet corner,—such as San Cassiano, where his estate was,—receiving daily intelligence from some sure friend, meanwhile, as to the turn matters were taking here—how, for instance, the Provost was not dead, after all, only wounded—or, as to-day's news would seem to prove, how Chiappino was not Brutus the Elder, after all, only the new Provost—and thus Luitolfo be enabled to watch a favorable opportunity for returning? Might it not have been so?

3rd BYSTANDER
Why, he may have taken that care of himself, certainly, for he came of a cautious stock. I'll tell you how his uncle, just such another gingerly treader on tiptoes with finger on lip,—how he met his death in the great plague-year: dico vobis! Hearing that the seventeenth house in a certain street was infected, he calculates to pass it in safety by taking plentiful breath, say, when he shall arrive at the eleventh house; then scouring by, holding that breath, till he be got so far on the other side as number twenty-three, and thus elude the danger.—And so did he begin; but, as he arrived at thirteen, we will say,—thinking to improve on his precaution by putting up a little prayer to Saint Nepomucene of Prague, this exhausted so much of his lungs' reserve, that at sixteen it was clean spent,—consequently at the fatal seventeen he inhaled with a vigor and persistence enough to suck you any latent venom out of the heart of a stone—Ha, ha!

LUITOLFO [Aside]

(If I had not lent that man the money he wanted last spring, I should fear this bitterness was attributable to me.) Luitolfo is dead then, one may conclude?

3rd BYSTANDER

Why, he had a house here, and a woman to whom he was affianced; and as they both pass naturally to the new Provost, his friend and heir ...

LUITOLFO

Ah, I suspected you of imposing on me with your pleasantry! I know Chiappino better.

1st BYSTANDER

(Our friend has the bile! After all, I do not dislike finding somebody vary a little this general gape of admiration at Chiappino's glorious qualities.) Pray, how much may you know of what has taken place in Faenza since that memorable night?

LUITOLFO

It is most to the purpose, that I know Chiappino to have been by profession a hater of that very office of Provost, you now charge him with proposing to accept.

1st BYSTANDER

Sir, I 'll tell you. That night was indeed memorable. Up we rose, a mass of us, men, women, children; out fled the guards with the body of the tyrant; we were to defy the world: but, next gray morning, "What will Rome say?" began everybody. You know we are governed by Ravenna, which is governed by Rome. And quietly into the town, by the Ravenna road, comes on muleback a portly personage, Ogniben by name, with the quality of Pontifical Legate; trots briskly through the streets humming a "Cur fremuere gentes," and makes directly for the Provost's Palace—there it faces you. "One Messer Chiappino is your leader? I have known three-and-twenty leaders of revolts!" (laughing gently to himself)—"Give me the help of your arm from my mule to yonder steps under the pillar—So! And now, my revolters and good friends, what do you want? The guards burst into Ravenna last night bearing your wounded Provost; and, having had a little talk with him, I take on myself to come and try appease the disorderliness, before Rome, hearing of it, resort to another method: 't is I come, and not another, from a certain love I confess to, of composing differences. So, do you understand, you are about to experience this unheard-of tyranny from me, that there shall be no heading nor hanging, nor confiscation nor exile: I insist on your simply pleasing yourselves. And now, pray, what does please you? To live without any government at all? Or having decided for one, to see its minister murdered by the first of your body that chooses to find himself wronged, or disposed for reverting to first principles and a justice anterior to all institutions,—and so will you carry matters, that the rest of the world must at length unite and put down such a den of wild beasts? As for vengeance on what has just taken place,—once for all, the wounded man assures me he cannot conjecture who struck him; and this so earnestly, that one may be sure he knows perfectly well what intimate acquaintance could find admission to speak with him late last evening. I come not for vengeance therefore, but from pure curiosity to hear what you will do next." And thus he ran on, on, easily and volubly, till he seemed to arrive quite naturally at the praise of law, order, and paternal government by somebody from rather a distance. All our citizens were in the snare, and about to be friends with so congenial an adviser; but that Chiappino suddenly stood forth, spoke out indignantly, and set things right again.

LUITOLFO

Do you see? I recognize him there!

3rd BYSTANDER

Ay, but, mark you, at the end of Chiappino's longest period in praise of a pure republic,—"And by whom do I desire such a government should be administered, perhaps, but by one like yourself?" returns the Legate: thereupon speaking for a quarter of an hour together, on the natural and only legitimate government by the best and wisest. And it should seem there was soon discovered to be no such vast discrepancy at bottom between this and Chiappino's theory, place but each in its proper light. "Oh, are you there?" quoth Chiappino: "Ay, in that, I agree," returns Chiappino: and so on.

LUITOLFO

But did Chiappino cede at once to this?

1st BYSTANDER

Why, not altogether at once. For instance, he said that the difference between him and all his fellows was, that they seemed all wishing to be kings in one or another way,—"whereas what right," asked he, "has any man to wish to be superior to another?"—whereat, "Ah, sir," answers the Legate, "this is the death of me, so often as I expect something is really going to be revealed to us by you clearer-seers, deeper-thinkers—this—that your right-hand (to speak by a figure) should be found taking up the weapon it displayed so ostentatiously, not to destroy any dragon in our path, as was prophesied, but simply to cut off its own fellow left-hand: yourself set about attacking yourself. For see now! Here are you who, I make sure, glory exceedingly in knowing the noble nature of the soul, its divine impulses, and so forth; and with such a knowledge you stand, as it were, armed to encounter the natural doubts and fears as to that same inherent nobility, which are apt to waylay us, the weaker ones, in the road of life. And when we look eagerly to see them fall before you, lo, round you wheel, only the left-hand gets the blow; one proof of the soul's nobility destroys simply another proof, quite as good, of the same, for you are found delivering an opinion like this! Why, what is this perpetual yearning to exceed, to subdue, to be better than, and a king over, one's fellows,—all that you so disclaim,—but the very tendency yourself are most proud of, and under another form, would oppose to it,—only in a lower stage of manifestation? You don't want to be vulgarly superior to your fellows after their poor fashion— to have me hold solemnly up your gown's tail, or hand you an express of the last importance from the Pope, with all these bystanders noticing how unconcerned you look the while: but neither does our gaping friend, the burgess yonder, want the other kind of kingship, that consists in understanding better than his fellows this and similar points of human nature, nor to roll under his tongue this sweeter morsel still, —the feeling that, through immense philosophy, he does not feel, he rather thinks, above you and me!" And so chatting, they glided off arm-in-arm.

LUITOLFO

And the result is ...

1st BYSTANDER

Why that, a month having gone by, the indomitable Chiappino, marrying as he will Luitolfo's love—at all events succeeding to Luitolfo's wealth—becomes the first inhabitant of Faenza, and a proper aspirant to the Provostship; which we assemble here to see conferred on him this morning. The Legate's Guard to clear the way! He will follow presently.

LUITOLFO [Withdrawing a little]

I understand the drift of Eulalia's communications less than ever. Yet she surely said, in so many words, that Chiappino was in urgent danger: wherefore, disregarding her injunction to continue in my retreat and await the result of—what she called, some experiment yet in process—I hastened here without her leave or knowledge: how could I else? But if this they say be true—if it were for such a purpose, she and Chiappino kept me away ... Oh, no, no! I must confront him and her before I believe this of them. And at the word, see!

[Enter **CHIAPPINO** and **EULALIA**.

EULALIA
We part here, then? The change in your principles would seem to be complete.

CHIAPPINO
Now, why refuse to see that in my present course I change no principles, only re-adapt them and more adroitly? I had despaired of what you may call the material instrumentality of life; of ever being able to rightly operate on mankind through such a deranged machinery as the existing modes of government: but now, if I suddenly discover how to inform these perverted institutions with fresh purpose, bring the functionary limbs once more into immediate communication with, and subjection to, the soul I am about to bestow on them—do you see? Why should one desire to invent, as long as it remains possible to renew and transform? When all further hope of the old organization shall be extinct, then, I grant you, it may be time to try and create another.

EULALIA
And there being discoverable some hope yet in the hitherto much-abused old system of absolute government by a Provost here, you mean to take your time about endeavoring to realize those visions of a perfect State we once heard of?

CHIAPPINO
Say, I would fain realize my conception of a palace, for instance, and that there is, abstractedly, but a single way of erecting one perfectly. Here, in the market-place is my allotted building-ground; here I stand without a stone to lay, or a laborer to help me,—stand, too, during a short day of life, close on which the night comes. On the other hand, circumstances suddenly offer me (turn and see it!) the old Provost's house to experiment upon—ruinous, if you please, wrongly constructed at the beginning, and ready to tumble now. But materials abound, a crowd of workmen offer their services; here exists yet a Hall of Audience of originally noble proportions, there a Guest-chamber of symmetrical design enough: and I may restore, enlarge, abolish or unite these to heart's content. Ought I not make the best of such an opportunity, rather than continue to gaze disconsolately with folded arms on the flat pavement here, while the sun goes slowly down, never to rise again? Since you cannot understand this nor me, it is better we should part as you desire.

EULALIA
So, the love breaks away too!

CHIAPPINO
No, rather my soul's capacity for love widens—needs more than one object to content it,—and, being better instructed, will not persist in seeing all the component parts of love in what is only a single part,—nor in finding that so many and so various loves are all united in the love of a woman,—manifold uses in one instrument, as the savage has his sword, staff, sceptre and idol, all in one club-stick. Love is a

very compound thing. The intellectual part of my love I shall give to men, the mighty dead or the illustrious living; and determine to call a mere sensual instinct by as few fine names as possible. What do I lose?

EULALIA
Nay, I only think, what do I lose? and, one more word—which shall complete my instruction—does friendship go too? What of Luitolfo, the author of your present prosperity?

CHIAPPINO
How the author?

EULALIA
That blow now called yours ...

CHIAPPINO
Struck without principle or purpose, as by a blind natural operation: yet to which all my thought and life directly and advisedly tended. I would have struck it, and could not: he would have done his utmost to avoid striking it, yet did so. I dispute his right to that deed of mine—a final action with him, from the first effect of which he fled away,—a mere first step with me, on which I base a whole mighty superstructure of good to follow. Could he get good from it?

EULALIA
So we profess, so we perform!

[Enter **OGNIBEN**. **EULALIA** stands apart.

OGNIBEN
I have seen three-and-twenty leaders of revolts. By your leave, sir! Perform? What does the lady say of performing?

CHIAPPINO
Only the trite saying, that we must not trust profession, only performance.

OGNIBEN
She 'll not say that, sir, when she knows you longer; you 'll instruct her better. Ever judge of men by their professions! For though the bright moment of promising is but a moment and cannot be prolonged, yet, if sincere in its moment's extravagant goodness, why, trust it and know the man by it, I say—not by his performance; which is half the world's work, interfere as the world needs must, with its accidents and circumstances: the profession was purely the man's own. I judge people by what they might be,—not are, nor will be.

CHIAPPINO
But have there not been found, too, performing natures, not merely promising?

OGNIBEN
Plenty. Little Bindo of our town, for instance, promised his friend, great ugly Masaccio, once, "I will repay you!"—for a favor done him. So, when his father came to die, and Bindo succeeded to the inheritance, he sends straightway for Masaccio and shares all with him—gives him half the land, half the

money, half the kegs of wine in the cellar. "Good," say you: and it is good. But had little Bindo found himself possessor of all this wealth some five years before—on the happy night when Masaccio procured him that interview in the garden with his pretty cousin Lisa —instead of being the beggar he then was,—I am bound to believe that in the warm moment of promise he would have given away all the wine-kegs and all the money and all the land, and only reserved to himself some hut on a hilltop hard by, whence he might spend his life in looking and seeing his friend enjoy himself: he meant fully that much, but the world interfered. —To our business! Did I understand you just now within-doors? You are not going to marry your old friend's love, after all?

CHIAPPINO

I must have a woman that can sympathize with, and appreciate me, I told you.

OGNIBEN

Oh, I remember! You, the greater nature, needs must have a lesser one (—avowedly lesser—contest with you on that score would never do)—such a nature must comprehend you, as the phrase is, accompany and testify of your greatness from point to point onward. Why, that were being not merely as great as yourself, but greater considerably! Meantime, might not the more bounded nature as reasonably count on your appreciation of it, rather?—on your keeping close by it, so far as you both go together, and then going on by yourself as far as you please? Thus God serves us.

CHIAPPINO

And yet a woman that could understand the whole of me, to whom I could reveal alike the strength and the weakness—

OGNIBEN

Ah, my friend, wish for nothing so foolish! Worship your love, give her the best of you to see; be to her like the western lands (they bring us such strange news of) to the Spanish Court; send her only your lumps of gold, fans of feathers, your spirit-like birds, and fruits and gems! So shall you, what is unseen of you, be supposed altogether a paradise by her,—as these western lands by Spain: though I warrant there is filth, red baboons, ugly reptiles and squalor enough, which they bring Spain as few samples of as possible. Do you want your mistress to respect your body generally? Offer her your mouth to kiss: don't strip off your boot and put your foot to her lips! You understand my humor by this time? I help men to carry out their own principles: if they please to say two and two make five, I assent, so they will but go on and say, four and four make ten.

CHIAPPINO

But these are my private affairs; what I desire you to occupy yourself about, is my public appearance presently: for when the people hear that I am appointed Provost, though you and I may thoroughly discern—and easily, too—the right principle at bottom of such a movement, and how my republicanism remains thoroughly unaltered, only takes a form of expression hitherto commonly judged (and heretofore by myself) incompatible with its existence,—when thus I reconcile myself to an old form of government instead of proposing a new one—

OGNIBEN

Why, you must deal with people broadly. Begin at a distance from this matter and say,—New truths, old truths! sirs, there is nothing new possible to be revealed to us in the moral world; we know all we shall ever know: and it is for simply reminding us, by their various respective expedients, how we do know this and the other matter, that men get called prophets, poets and the like. A philosopher's life is spent in discovering that, of the half-dozen truths he knew when a child, such an one is a lie, as the world states it in set terms; and then, after a weary lapse of years, and plenty of hard thinking, it becomes a truth again after all, as he happens to newly consider it and view it in a different relation with the others: and so he re-states it, to the confusion of somebody else in good time. As for adding to the original stock of truths,—impossible! Thus, you see the expression of them is the grand business:—you have got a truth in your head about the right way of governing people, and you took a mode of expressing it which now you confess to be imperfect. But what then? There is truth in falsehood, falsehood in truth. No man ever told one great truth, that I know, without the help of a good dozen of lies at least, generally unconscious ones. And as when a child comes in breathlessly and relates a strange story, you try to conjecture from the very falsities in it what the reality was,—do not conclude that he saw nothing in the sky, because he assuredly did not see a flying horse there as he says,—so, through the contradictory expression, do you see, men should look painfully for, and trust to arrive eventually at, what you call the true principle at bottom. Ah, what an answer is there! to what will it not prove applicable?—"Contradictions? Of course there were," say you!

CHIAPPINO
Still, the world at large may call it inconsistency, and what shall I urge in reply?

OGNIBEN
Why, look you, when they tax you with tergiversation or duplicity, you may answer—you begin to perceive that, when all 's done and said, both great parties in the State, the advocators of change in the present system of things, and the opponents of it, patriot and anti-patriot, are found working together for the common good; and that in the midst of their efforts for and against its progress, the world somehow or other still advances: to which result they contribute in equal proportions, those who spend their life in pushing it onward, as those who give theirs to the business of pulling it back. Now, if you found the world stand still between the opposite forces, and were glad, I should conceive you: but it steadily advances, you rejoice to see! By the side of such a rejoicer, the man who only winks as he keeps cunning and quiet, and says, "Let yonder hot-headed fellow fight out my battle! I, for one, shall win in the end by the blows he gives, and which I ought to be giving,"—even he seems graceful in his avowal, when one considers that he might say, "I shall win quite as much by the blows our antagonist gives him, blows from which he saves me—I thank the antagonist equally!" Moreover, you may enlarge on the loss of the edge of party-animosity with age and experience ...

CHIAPPINO
And naturally time must wear off such asperities: the bitterest adversaries get to discover certain points of similarity between each other, common sympathies—do they not?

OGNIBEN
Ay, had the young David but sat first to dine on his cheeses with the Philistine, he had soon discovered an abundance of such common sympathies. He of Gath, it is recorded, was born of a father and mother, had brothers and sisters like another man,—they, no more than the sons of Jesse, were used to eat each other. But, for the sake of one broad antipathy that had existed from the beginning, David slung the stone, cut off the giant's head, made a spoil of it, and after ate his cheeses alone, with the better appetite, for all I can learn. My friend, as you, with a quickened eyesight, go on discovering much good on the worse side, remember that the same process should proportionally magnify and demonstrate to you the much more good on the better side! And when I profess no sympathy for the Goliaths of our time, and you object that a large nature should sympathize with every form of intelligence, and see the good in it, however limited,—I answer, "So I do; but preserve the proportions of my sympathy, however

finelier or widelier I may extend its action." I desire to be able, with a quickened eyesight, to descry beauty in corruption where others see foulness only; but I hope I shall also continue to see a redoubled beauty in the higher forms of matter, where already everybody sees no foulness at all. I must retain, too, my old power of selection, and choice of appropriation, to apply to such new gifts; else they only dazzle instead of enlightening me. God has his archangels and consorts with them: though he made too, and intimately sees what is good in, the worm. Observe, I speak only as you profess to think and so ought to speak: I do justice to your own principles, that is all.

CHIAPPINO

But you very well know that the two parties do, on occasion, assume each other's characteristics. What more disgusting, for instance, than to see how promptly the newly emancipated slave will adopt, in his own favor, the very measures of precaution, which pressed soreliest on himself as institutions of the tyranny he has just escaped from? Do the classes, hitherto without opinion, get leave to express it? there follows a confederacy immediately, from which—exercise your individual right and dissent, and woe be to you!

OGNIBEN

And a journey over the sea to you! That is the generous way. Cry—"Emancipated slaves, the first excess, and off I go!" The first time a poor devil, who has been bastinadoed steadily his whole life long, finds himself let alone and able to legislate, so, begins pettishly, while he rubs his soles, "Woe be to whoever brings anything in the shape of a stick this way!"—you, rather than give up the very innocent pleasure of carrying one to switch flies with,—you go away, to everybody's sorrow. Yet you were quite reconciled to staying at home while the governors used to pass, every now and then, some such edict as, "Let no man indulge in owning a stick which is not thick enough to chastise our slaves, if need require!" Well, there are pre-ordained hierarchies among us, and a profane vulgar subjected to a different law altogether; yet I am rather sorry you should see it so clearly: for, do you know what is to—all but save you at the Day of Judgment, all you men of genius? It is this: that, while you generally began by pulling down God, and went on to the end of your life in one effort at setting up your own genius in his place,—still, the last, bitterest concession wrung with the utmost unwillingness from the experience of the very loftiest of you, was invariably—would one think it?—that the rest of mankind, down to the lowest of the mass, stood not, nor ever could stand, just on a level and equality with yourselves. That will be a point in the favor of all such, I hope and believe.

CHIAPPINO

Why, men of genius are usually charged, I think, with doing just the reverse; and at once acknowledging the natural inequality of mankind, by themselves participating in the universal craving after, and deference to, the civil distinctions which represent it. You wonder they pay such undue respect to titles and badges of superior rank.

OGNIBEN

Not I (always on your own ground and showing, be it noted!) Who doubts that, with a weapon to brandish, a man is the more formidable? Titles and badges are exercised as such a weapon, to which you and I look up wistfully. We could pin lions with it moreover, while in its present owner's hands it hardly prods rats. Nay, better than a mere weapon of easy mastery and obvious use, it is a mysterious divining-rod that may serve us in undreamed-of ways. Beauty, strength, intellect—men often have none of these, and yet conceive pretty accurately what kind of advantages they would bestow on the possessor. We know at least what it is we make up our mind to forego, and so can apply the fittest substitute in our power. Wanting beauty, we cultivate good-humor; missing wit, we get riches: but the mystic unimaginable operation of that gold collar and string of Latin names which suddenly turned poor stupid little peevish Cecco of our town into natural lord of the best of us—a Duke, he is now—there indeed is a virtue to be reverenced!

CHIAPPINO
Ay, by the vulgar: not by Messere Stiatta the poet, who pays more assiduous court to him than anybody.

OGNIBEN
What else should Stiatta pay court to? He has talent, not honor and riches: men naturally covet what they have not.

CHIAPPINO
No; or Cecco would covet talent, which he has not, whereas he covets more riches, of which he has plenty, already.

OGNIBEN
Because a purse added to a purse makes the holder twice as rich: but just such another talent as Stiatta's, added to what he now possesses, what would that profit him? Give the talent a purse indeed, to do something with! But lo, how we keep the good people waiting! I only desired to do justice to the noble sentiments which animate you, and which you are too modest to duly enforce. Come, to our main business: shall we ascend the steps? I am going to propose you for Provost to the people; they know your antecedents, and will accept you with a joyful unanimity: whereon I confirm their choice. Rouse up! Are you nerving yourself to an effort? Beware the disaster of Messere Stiatta we were talking of! who, determining to keep an equal mind and constant face on whatever might be the fortune of his last new poem with our townsmen, heard too plainly "hiss, hiss, hiss," increase every moment. Till at last the man fell senseless: not perceiving that the portentous sounds had all the while been issuing from between his own nobly clenched teeth, and nostrils narrowed by resolve.

CHIAPPINO
Do you begin to throw off the mask?—to jest with me, having got me effectually into your trap?

OGNIBEN
Where is the trap, my friend? You hear what I engage to do, for my part: you, for yours, have only to fulfil your promise made just now within doors, of professing unlimited obedience to Rome's authority in my person. And I shall authorize no more than the simple re-establishment of the Provostship and the conferment of its privileges upon yourself: the only novel stipulation being a birth of the peculiar circumstances of the time.

CHIAPPINO
And that stipulation?

OGNIBEN
Just the obvious one—that in the event of the discovery of the actual assailant of the late Provost ...

CHIAPPINO
Ha!

OGNIBEN

Why, he shall suffer the proper penalty, of course; what did you expect?

CHIAPPINO
Who heard of this?

OGNIBEN
Rather, who needed to hear of this?

CHIAPPINO
Can it be, the popular rumor never reached you ...

OGNIBEN
Many more such rumors reach me, friend, than I choose to receive: those which wait longest have best chance. Has the present one sufficiently waited? Now is its time for entry with effect. See the good people crowding about yonder palace-steps—which we may not have to ascend, after all! My good friends! (nay, two or three of you will answer every purpose)—who was it fell upon and proved nearly the death of your late Provost? His successor desires to hear, that his day of inauguration may be graced by the act of prompt, bare justice we all anticipate. Who dealt the blow that night, does anybody know?

LUITOLFO [Coming forward]
I!

ALL
Luitolfo!

LUITOLFO
I avow the deed, justify and approve it, and stand forth now, to relieve my friend of an unearned responsibility. Having taken thought, I am grown stronger: I shall shrink from nothing that awaits me. Nay, Chiappino—we are friends still: I dare say there is some proof of your superior nature in this starting aside, strange as it seemed at first. So, they tell me, my horse is of the right stock, because a shadow in the path frightens him into a frenzy, makes him dash my brains out. I understand only the dull mule's way of standing stockishly, plodding soberly, suffering on occasion a blow or two with due patience.

EULALIA
I was determined to justify my choice, Chiappino; to let Luitolfo's nature vindicate itself. Henceforth we are undivided, whatever be our fortune.

OGNIBEN
Now, in these last ten minutes of silence, what have I been doing, deem you? Putting the finishing stroke to a homily of mine, I have long taken thought to perfect, on the text, "Let whoso thinketh he standeth, take heed lest he fall." To your house, Luitolfo! Still silent, my patriotic friend? Well, that is a good sign however. And you will go aside for a time? That is better still. I understand: it would be easy for you to die of remorse here on the spot and shock us all, but you mean to live and grow worthy of coming back to us one day. There, I will tell everybody; and you only do right to believe you must get better as you get older. All men do so: they are worst in childhood, improve in manhood, and get ready in old age for another world. Youth, with its beauty and grace, would seem bestowed on us for some such reason as to make us partly endurable till we have time for really becoming so of ourselves,

without their aid; when they leave us. The sweetest child we all smile on for his pleasant want of the whole world to break up, or suck in his mouth, seeing no other good in it—would be rudely handled by that world's inhabitants, if he retained those angelic infantine desires when he had grown six feet high, black and bearded. But, little by little, he sees fit to forego claim after claim on the world, puts up with a less and less share of its good as his proper portion; and when the octogenarian asks barely a sup of gruel and a fire of dry sticks, and thanks you as for his full allowance and right in the common good of life,—hoping nobody may murder him,—he who began by asking and expecting the whole of us to bow down in worship to him,—why, I say he is advanced, far onward, very far, nearly out of sight like our friend Chiappino yonder. And now—(ay, good-by to you! He turns round the northwest gate: going to Lugo again? Good-by!)—And now give thanks to God, the keys of the Provost's palace to me, and yourselves to profitable meditation at home! I have known Four-and-twenty leaders of revolts.

LURIA

A TRAGEDY

I DEDICATE THIS LAST ATTEMPT FOR THE PRESENT AT DRAMATIC POETRY TO A GREAT DRAMATIC POET; "WISHING WHAT I WRITE MAY BE READ BY HIS LIGHT:" IF A PHRASE ORIGINALLY ADDRESSED, BY NOT THE LEAST WORTHY OF HIS CONTEMPORARIES, TO SHAKESPEARE, MAY BE APPLIED HERE, BY ONE WHOSE SOLE PRIVILEGE IS IN A GRATEFUL ADMIRATION, To WALTER SAVAGE LANDOR

LONDON, 1846.

PERSONS
LURIA, a Moor, Commander of the Florentine Forces.
HUSAIN, a Moor, his friend.
PUCCIO, the old Florentine Commander, now LURIA'S Chief Officer.
BRACCIO, Commissary of the Republic of Florence.
JACOPO (LAPO), his Secretary.
TIBURZIO, Commander of the Pisans.
DOMIZIA, a noble Florentine Lady.

TIME: 14—.

SCENE: Luria's Camp between Florence and Pisa.

ACT I

MORNING

BRACCIO, as dictating to his **SECRETARY**; **PUCCIO** standing by.

BRACCIO [To **PUCCIO**]
Then, you join battle in an hour?

PUCCIO
Not I;
Luria, the captain.

BRACCIO
[To the **SECRETARY**] "In an hour, the battle."
[To **PUCCIO**] Sir, let your eye run o'er this loose digest,
And see if very much of your report
Have slipped away through my civilian phrase.
Does this instruct the Signory aright
How army stands with army?

PUCCIO [Taking the paper]
All seems here:
—That Luria, seizing with our city's force
The several points of vantage, hill and plain,
Shuts Pisa safe from help on every side,
And, baffling the Lucchese arrived too late,
Must, in the battle he delivers now,
Beat her best troops and first of chiefs.

BRACCIO
So sure?
Tiburzio 's a consummate captain too!

PUCCIO
Luria holds Pisa's fortune in his hand.

BRACCIO [To the **SECRETARY**]
"The Signory hold Pisa in their hand."
Your own proved soldiership 's our warrant, sir:
So, while my secretary ends his task,
Have out two horsemen, by the open roads,
To post with it to Florence!

PUCCIO [Returning the paper]
All seems here;
Unless ... Ser Braccio, 't is my last report!
Since Pisa's outbreak, and my overthrow,
And Luria's hastening at the city's call
To save her, as he only could, no doubt;
Till now that she is saved or sure to be,—
Whatever you tell Florence, I tell you:
Each day's note you, her Commissary, make

Of Luria's movements, I myself supply.
No youngster am I longer, to my cost;
Therefore while Florence gloried in her choice
And vaunted Luria, whom but Luria, still,
As if zeal, courage, prudence, conduct, faith,
Had never met in any man before,
I saw no pressing need to swell the cry.
But now, this last report and I have done:
So, ere to-night comes with its roar of praise,
'T were not amiss if some one old i' the trade
Subscribed with, "True, for once rash counsel 's best.
This Moor of the bad faith and doubtful race,
This boy to whose untried sagacity,
Raw valor, Florence trusts without reserve
The charge to save her,—justifies her choice;
In no point has this stranger failed his friends.
Now praise!" I say this, and it is not here.

BRACCIO [To the **SECRETARY**]
Write, "Puccio, superseded in the charge,
By Luria, bears full witness to his worth,
Aid no reward our Signory can give
Their champion but he 'll back it cheerfully."
Aught more? Five minutes hence, both messengers!

[**PUCCIO** goes.

BRACCIO [After a pause, and while he slowly tears the paper into shreds.]
I think ... (pray God, I hold in fit contempt
This warfare 's noble art and ordering,
And,—once the brace of prizers fairly matched,
Poleaxe with poleaxe, knife with knife as good,—
Spit properly at what men term their skill!—)
Yet here I think our fighter has the odds.
With Pisa's strength diminished thus and thus,
Such points of vantage in our hands and such,
Lucca still off the stage, too,—all 's assured:
Luria must win this battle. Write the Court,
That Luria's trial end and sentence pass!

SECRETARY
Patron,—

BRACCIO
Ay, Lapo?

SECRETARY
If you trip, I fall;

'T is in self-interest I speak—

BRACCIO
Nay, nay,
You overshoot the mark, my Lapo! Nay!
When did I say pure love 's impossible?
I make you daily write those red cheeks thin,
Load your young brow with what concerns it least,
And, when we visit Florence, let you pace
The Piazza by my side as if we talked,
Where all your old acquaintances may see:
You 'd die for me, I should not be surprised.
Now then!

SECRETARY
Sir, look about and love yourself!
Step after step, the Signory and you
Tread gay till this tremendous point 's to pass;
Which pass not, pass not, ere you ask yourself,—
Bears the brain steadily such draughts of fire,
Or too delicious may not prove the pride
Of this long secret trial you dared plan,
Dare execute, you solitary here,
With the gray-headed toothless fools at home,
Who think themselves your lords, such slaves are they?
If they pronounce this sentence as you bid,
Declare the treason, claim its penalty,—
And sudden out of all the blaze of life,
On the best minute of his brightest day,
From that adoring army at his back,
Through Florence' joyous crowds before his face,
Into the dark you beckon Luria ...

BRACCIO
Then—
Why, Lapo, when the fighting-people vaunt,
We of the other craft and mystery,
May we not smile demure, the danger past?

SECRETARY
Sir, no, no, no,—the danger, and your spirit
At watch and ward? Where 's danger on your part,
With that thin flitting instantaneous steel
'Gainst the blind bull-front of a brute-force world?
If Luria, that 's to perish sure as fate,
Should have been really guiltless after all?

BRACCIO

Ah, you have thought that?

SECRETARY
Here I sit, your scribe,
And in and out goes Luria, days and nights;
This Puccio comes; the Moor his other friend,
Husain; they talk—that 's all feigned easily;
He speaks (I would not listen if I could),
Reads, orders, counsels:—but he rests sometimes,—
I see him stand and eat, sleep stretched an hour
On the lynx-skins yonder; hold his bared black arms
Into the sun from the tent-opening; laugh
When his horse drops the forage from his teeth
And neighs to hear him hum his Moorish songs.
That man believes in Florence, as the saint
Tied to the wheel believes in God.

BRACCIO
How strange!
You too have thought that!

SECRETARY
Do but you think too,
And all is saved! I only have to write,
"The man seemed false awhile, proves true at last;
Bury it"—so I write the Signory—
"Bury this trial in your breast forever,
Blot it from things or done or dreamed about!
So Luria shall receive his meed to-day
With no suspicion what reverse was near,—
As if no meteoric finger hushed
The doom-word just on the destroyer's lip,
Motioned him off, and let life's sun fall straight."

BRACCIO [Looks to the wall of the tent]
Did he draw that?

SECRETARY
With charcoal, when the watch
Made the report at midnight; Lady Domizia
Spoke of the unfinished Duomo, you remember,
That is his fancy how a Moorish front
Might join to, and complete, the body,—a sketch,—
And again where the cloak hangs, yonder in the shadow.

BRACCIO
He loves that woman.

SECRETARY

She is sent the spy
Of Florence,—spies on you as you on him:
Florence, if only for Domizia's sake,
Is surely safe. What shall I write?

BRACCIO

I see—
A Moorish front, nor of such ill design!
Lapo, there 's one thing plain and positive;
Man seeks his own good at the whole world's cost.
What? If to lead our troops, stand forth out chiefs,
And hold our fate, and see us at their beck,
Yet render up the charge when peace return,
Have ever proved too much for Florentines,
Even for the best and bravest of ourselves—
If in the struggle when the soldier's sword
Should sink its point before the statist's pen,
And the calm head replace the violent hand,
Virtue on virtue still have fallen away
Before ambition with unvarying fate,
Till Florence' self at last in bitterness
Be forced to own such falls the natural end,
And, sparing further to expose her sons
To a vain strife and profitless disgrace,
Declare, "The foreigner, one not my child,
Shall henceforth lead my troops, reach height by height
The glory, then descend into the shame;
So shall rebellion be less guilt in him,
And punishment the easier task for me:"
—If on the best of us such brand she set,
Can I suppose an utter alien here,
This Luria, our inevitable foe,
Confessed a mercenary and a Moor,
Born free from many ties that bind the rest
Of common faith in Heaven or hope on earth,
No past with us, no future,—such a spirit
Shall hold the path from which our stanchest broke,
Stand firm where every famed precursor fell?
My Lapo, I will frankly say, these proofs
So duly noted of the man's intent,
Are for the doting fools at home, not me.
The charges here, they may be true or false:
—What is set down? Errors and oversights,
A dallying interchange of courtesies
With Pisa's General,—all that, hour by hour,
Puccio's pale discontent has furnished us,
Of petulant speeches, inconsiderate acts,

Now overhazard, overcaution now;
Even that he loves this lady who believes
She outwits Florence, and whom Florence posted
By my procurement here, to spy on me,
Lest I one minute lose her from my sight—
She who remembering her whole House's fall,
That nest of traitors strangled in the birth,
Now labors to make Luria (poor device
As plain) the instrument of her revenge!
—That she is ever at his ear to prompt
Inordinate conceptions of his worth,
Exorbitant belief in worth's reward,
And after, when sure disappointment follows,
Proportionable rage at such a wrong—
Why, all these reasons, while I urge them most,
Weigh with me less than least; as nothing weigh.
Upon that broad man's-heart of his, I go:
On what I know must be, yet while I live
Shall never be, because I live and know.
Brute-force shall not rule Florence! Intellect
May rule her, bad or good as chance supplies:
But intellect it shall be, pure if bad,
And intellect's tradition so kept up!
Till the good come—'t was intellect that ruled,
Not brute-force bringing from the battlefield
The attributes of wisdom, foresight's graces
We lent it there to lure its grossness on;
All which it took for earnest and kept safe
To show against us in our market-place,
Just as the plumes and tags and swordsman's-gear
(Fetched from the camp where, at their foolish best,
When all was done they frightened nobody)
Perk in our faces in the street, forsooth,
With our own warrant and allowance. No!
The whole procedure's overcharged,—its end
In too strict keeping with the bad first step.
To conquer Pisa was sheer inspiration?
Well then, to perish for a single fault,
Let that be simple justice! There, my Lapo!
A Moorish front ill suits our Duomo's body:
Blot it out—and bid Luria's sentence come!

[**LURIA**, who, with **DOMIZIA**, has entered unobserved at the close of the last phrase, now advances.

LURIA
And Luria, Luria, what of Luria now?

BRACCIO

Ah, you so close, sir? Lady Domizia too?
I said it needs must be a busy moment
For one like you; that you were now i' the thick
Of your duties, doubtless, while we idlers sat ...

LURIA
No—in that paper,—it was in that paper
What you were saving!

BRACCIO
Oh—my day's despatch!
I censure you to Florence: will you see?

LURIA
See your despatch, your last, for the first time?
Well, if I should, now? For in truth, Domizia,
He would be forced to set about another,
In his sly cool way, the true Florentine,
To mention that important circumstance.
So, while he wrote I should gain time, such time!
Do not send this!

BRACCIO
And wherefore?

LURIA
These Lucchese
Are not arrived—they never will arrive!
And I must fight to-day, arrived or not,
And I shall beat Tiburzio, that is sure:
And then will be arriving his Lucchese,
But slowly, oh so slowly, just in time
To look upon my battle from the hills,
Like a late moon, of use to nobody!
And I must break my battle up, send forth,
Surround on this side, hold in check on that.
Then comes to-morrow, we negotiate,
You make me send for fresh instructions home,
—Incompleteness, incompleteness!

BRACCIO
Ah, we scribes!
Why, I had registered that very point,
The non-appearance of our foes' ally,
As a most happy fortune; both at once
Were formidable: singly faced, each falls.

LURIA

So, no great battle for my Florentines!
No crowning deed, decisive and complete,
For all of them, the simple as the wise,
Old, young, alike, that do not understand
Our wearisome pedantic art of war,
By which we prove retreat may be success,
Delay—best speed,—half loss, at times,—whole gain:
They want results: as if it were their fault!
And you, with warmest wish to be my friend,
Will not be able now to simply say
"Your servant has performed his task—enough!
You ordered, he has executed: good!
Now walk the streets in holiday attire,
Congratulate your friends, till noon strikes fierce,
Then form bright groups beneath the Duomo's shade!"
No, you will have to argue and explain,
Persuade them, all is not so ill in the end,
Tease, tire them out! Arrive, arrive, Lucchese!

DOMIZIA

Well, you will triumph for the past enough,
Whatever be the present chance; no service
Falls to the ground with Florence: she awaits
Her savior, will receive him fittingly.

LURIA

Ah, Braccio, you know Florence! Will she, think you,
Receive one ... what means "fittingly receive"?
—Receive compatriots, doubtless—I am none:
And yet Domizia promises so much!

BRACCIO

Kind women still give men a woman's prize.
I know not o'er which gate most boughs will arch.
Nor if the Square will wave red flags or blue.
I should have judged, the fullest of rewards
Our state gave Luria, when she made him chief
Of her whole force, in her best captain's place.

LURIA

That, my reward? Florence on my account
Relieved Ser Puccio?—mark you, my reward!
And Puccio's having all the fight's true joy—
Goes here and there, gets close, may fight, himself,
While I must order, stand aloof, o'ersee.
That was my calling, there was my true place!
I should have felt, in some one over me,
Florence impersonate, my visible head,

As I am over Puccio,—taking life
Directly from her eye! They give me you:
But do you cross me, set me half to work?
I enjoy nothing—though I will, for once!
Decide, shall we join battle? may I wait?

BRACCIO
Let us compound the matter; wait till noon:
Then, no arrival,—

LURIA
Ah, noon comes too fast!
I wonder, do you guess why I delay
Involuntarily the final blow
As long as possible? Peace follows it!
Florence at peace, and the calm studious heads
Come out again, the penetrating eyes;
As if a spell broke, all 's resumed, each art
You boast, more vivid that it slept awhile.
'Gainst the glad heaven, o'er the white palace-front
The interrupted scaffold climbs anew;
The walls are peopled by the painter's brush;
The statue to its niche ascends to dwell.
The present noise and trouble have retired
And left the eternal past to rule once more;
You speak its speech and read its records plain,
Greece lives with you, each Roman breathes your friend:
But Luria—where will then be Luria's place?

DOMIZIA
Highest in honor, for that past's own sake,
Of which his actions, sealing up the sum
By saving all that went before from wreck,
Will range as part, with which be worshipped too.

LURIA
Then I may walk and watch you in your streets,
Lead the smooth life my rough life helps no more,
So different, so new, so beautiful—
Nor fear that you will tire to see parade
The club that slew the lion, now that crooks
And shepherd-pipes come into use again?
For very lone and silent seems my East
In its drear vastness: still it spreads, and still
No Braccios, no Domizias anywhere—
Not ever more! Well, well, to-day is ours!

DOMIZIA [To **BRACCIO**]

Should he not have been one of us?

LURIA
Oh, no!
Not one of you, and so escape the thrill
Of coming into you, of changing thus,—
Feeling a soul grow on me that restricts
The boundless unrest of the savage heart!
The sea heaves up, hangs loaded o'er the land,
Breaks there and buries its tumultuous strength;
Horror, and silence, and a pause awhile:
Lo, inland glides the gulf-stream, miles away,
In rapture of assent, subdued and still,
'Neath those strange banks, those unimagined skies.
Well, 't is not sure the quiet lasts forever!
Your placid heads still find rough hands new work;
Some minute's chance—there comes the need of mine:
And, all resolved on, I too hear at last.
Oh, you must find some use for me, Ser Braccio!
You hold my strength; 't were best dispose of it:
What you created, see that you find food for—
I shall be dangerous else!

BRACCIO
How dangerous, sir?

LURIA
There are so many ways, Domizia warns me,
And one with half the power that I possess,
—Grows very formidable! Do you doubt?
Why, first, who holds the army ...

DOMIZIA
While we talk,
Morn wears; we keep you from your proper place,
The field.

LURIA
Nay, to the field I move no more;
My part is done, and Puccio's may begin:
I cannot trench upon his province longer
With any face.—You think yourselves so safe?
Why, see—in concert with Tiburzio, now—
One could ...

DOMIZIA
A trumpet!

LURIA
My Lucchese at last!
Arrived, as sure as Florence stands! Your leave!

[Springs out.

DOMIZIA
How plainly is true greatness charactered
By such unconscious sport as Luria's here,
Strength sharing least the secret of itself!
Be it with head that schemes or hand that acts,
Such save the world which none but they could save,
Yet think whate'er they did, that world could do.

BRACCIO
Yes: and how worthy note, that these same great ones
In hand or head, with such unconsciousness
And all its due entailed humility,
Should never shrink, so far as I perceive,
From taking up whatever tool there be
Effects the whole world's safety or mishap,
Into their mild hands as a thing of course!
The statist finds it natural to lead
The mob who might as easily lead him—
The captain marshals troops born skilled in war—
Statist and captain verily believe!
While we poor scribes ... you catch me thinking now,
That I shall in this very letter write
What none of you are able! To it, Lapo!

[**DOMIZIA** goes.

This last worst all-affected childish fit
Of Luria's, this be-praised unconsciousness,
Convinces me; the past was no child's play:
It was a man beat Pisa,—not a child.
All 's mere dissimulation—to remove
The fear, he best knows we should entertain.
The utmost danger was at hand. Is 't written?
Now make a duplicate, lest this should fail,
And speak your fullest on the other side.

SECRETARY
I noticed he was busily repairing
My half-effacement of his Duomo sketch,
And, while he spoke of Florence, turned to it,
As the Mage Negro king to Christ the babe.
I judge his childishness the mere relapse

To boyhood of a man who has worked lately,
And presently will work, so, meantime, plays:
Whence, more than ever I believe in him.

BRACCIO [After a pause]
The sword! At best, the soldier, as he says,
In Florence—the black face, the barbarous name,
For Italy to boast her show of the age,
Her man of men!—To Florence with each letter!

ACT II

NOON

DOMIZIA
Well, Florence, shall I reach thee, pierce thy heart
Through all its safeguards? Hate is said to help—
Quicken the eye, invigorate the arm;
And this my hate, made up of many hates,
Might stand in scorn of visible instrument,
And will thee dead: yet do I trust it not.
Nor man's devices nor Heaven's memory
Of wickedness forgot on earth so soon,
But thy own nature,—hell and thee I trust,
To keep thee constant in that wickedness,
Where my revenge may meet thee. Turn aside
A single step, for gratitude or shame,—
Grace but this Luria,—this wild mass of rage
I have prepared to launch against thee now,—
With other payment than thy noblest found,—
Give his desert for once its due reward,—
And past thee would my sure destruction roll.
But thou, who mad'st our House thy sacrifice,
It cannot be thou wilt except this Moor
From the accustomed fate of zeal and truth:
Thou wilt deny his looked-for recompense,
And then—I reach thee. Old and trained, my sire
Could bow down on his quiet broken heart,
Die awe-struck and submissive, when at last
The strange blow came for the expected wreath;
And Porzio passed in blind bewilderment
To exile, never to return,—they say,
Perplexed in his frank simple honest soul,
As if some natural law had changed,—how else
Could Florence, on plain fact pronouncing thus,
Judge Porzio's actions worthy such reward?

But Berto, with the ever-passionate pulse,
—Oh that long night, its dreadful hour on hour,
In which no way of getting his fair fame
From their inexplicable charges free,
Was found, save pouring forth the impatient blood
To show its color whether false or no!
My brothers never had a friend like me
Close in their need to watch the time, then speak,
—Burst with a wakening laughter on their dream,
Cry, "Florence was all falseness, so, false here!"
And show them what a simple task remained—
To leave dreams, rise, and punish in God's name
The city wedded to the wickedness.
None stood by them as I by Luria stand.
So, when the stranger cheated of his due
Turns on thee as his rapid nature bids,
Then, Florence, think, a hireling at thy throat
For the first outrage, think who bore thy last,
Yet mutely in forlorn obedience died!
He comes—his friend—black faces in the camp
Where moved those peerless brows and eyes of old.

[Enter **LURIA** and **HUSAIN**.

Well, and the movement—is it as you hope?
'T is Lucca?

LURIA
Ah, the Pisan trumpet merely!
Tiburzio's envoy, I must needs receive.

DOMIZIA
Whom I withdraw before; though if I lingered
You could not wonder, for my time fleets fast.
The overtaking night brings such reward!
And where will then be room for me? Yet, praised,
Remember who was first to promise praise,
And envy those who also can perform!

[Goes.

LURIA
This trumpet from the Pisans?—

HUSAIN
In the camp;
A very noble presence—Braccio's visage
On Puccio's body—calm and fixed and good;

A man I seem as I had seen before:
Most like, it was some statue had the face.

LURIA

Admit him! This will prove the last delay.

HUSAIN

Ay, friend, go on, and die thou going on!
Thou heard'st what the grave woman said but now:
To-night rewards thee. That is well to hear;
But stop not therefore: hear it, and go on!

LURIA

Oh, their reward and triumph and the rest
They round me in the ears with, all day long?
All that, I never take for earnest, friend!
Well would it suit us,—their triumphal arch
Or storied pillar,—thee and me, the Moors!
But gratitude in those Italian eyes—
That, we shall get?

HUSAIN

It is too cold an air.
Our sun rose out of yonder mound of mist:
Where is he now? So, I trust none of them.

LURIA

Truly?

HUSAIN

I doubt and fear. There stands a wall
'Twixt our expansive and explosive race
And those absorbing, concentrating men.
They use thee.

LURIA

And I feel it, Husain! yes,
And care not—yes, an alien force like mine
Is only called to play its part outside
Their different nature; where its sole use seems
To fight with and keep off an adverse force,
As alien,—which repelled, mine too withdraws:
Inside, they know not what to do with me.
Thus I have told them laughingly and oft,
But longsince am prepared to learn the worst.

HUSAIN

What is the worst?

LURIA

I will forestall them, Husain,
Will speak the destiny they dare not speak—
Banish myself before they find the heart.
I will be first to say, "The work rewards!
I know, for all your praise, my use is over,
So may it prove!—meanwhile 't is best I go,
Go carry safe my memories of you all
To other scenes of action, newer lands."—
Thus leaving them confirmed in their belief
They would not easily have tired of me.
You think this hard to say?

HUSAIN

Say or not say,
So thou but go, so they but let thee go!
This hating people, that hate each the other,
And in one blandness to us Moors unite—
Locked each to each like slippery snakes, I say,
Which still in all their tangles, hissing tongue
And threatening tail, ne'er do each other harm;
While any creature of a better blood,
They seem to fight for, while they circle safe
And never touch it,—pines without a wound,
Withers away beside their eyes and breath.
See thou, if Puccio come not safely out
Of Braccio's grasp, this Braccio sworn his foe,
As Braccio safely from Domizia's toils
Who hates him most! But thou, the friend of all,
... Come out of them!

LURIA

The Pisan trumpet now!

HUSAIN

Breathe free—it is an enemy, no friend!

[Goes.

LURIA

He keeps his instincts, no new culture mars
Their perfect use in him; just so the brutes
Rest not, are anxious without visible cause,
When change is in the elements at work,
Which man's trained senses fail to apprehend.
But here,—he takes the distant chariot-wheel
For thunder, festal flame for lightning's flash,

The finer traits of cultivated life
For treachery and malevolence: I see!

[Enter **TIBURZIO**.

LURIA
Quick, sir, your message! I but wait your message
To sound the charge. You bring no overture
For truce?—I would not, for your General's sake,
You spoke of truce: a time to fight is come,
And, whatsoe'er the fight's event, he keeps
His honest soldier's-name to heat me with,
Or leaves me all himself to beat, I trust!

TIBURZIO
I am Tiburzio.

LURIA
You? 'T is—yes ... Tiburzio!
You were the last to keep the ford i' the valley
From Puccio, when I threw in succors there!
Why, I was on the heights—through the defile
Ten minutes after, when the prey was lost!
You wore an open skull-cap with a twist
Of water-reeds—the plume being hewn away;
While I drove down my battle from the heights,
I saw with my own eyes!

TIBURZIO
And you are Luria
Who sent my cohort, that laid down its arms
In error of the battle-signal's sense,
Back safely to me at the critical time—
One of a hundred deeds. I know you! Therefore
To none but you could I ...

LURIA
No truce, Tiburzio!

TIBURZIO
Luria, you know the peril imminent
On Pisa,—that you have us in the toils,
Us her last safeguard, all that intercepts
The rage of her implacablest of foes
From Pisa: if we fall to-day, she falls.
Though Lucca will arrive, yet, 't is too late.
You have so plainly here the best of it,
That you must feel, brave soldier as you are,

How dangerous we grow in this extreme,
How truly formidable by despair.
Still, probabilities should have their weight:
The extreme chance is ours, but, that chance failing,
You win this battle. Wherefore say I this?
To be well apprehended when I add,
This danger absolutely comes from you.
Were you, who threaten thus, a Florentine ...

LURIA
Sir, I am nearer Florence than her sons.
I can, and have perhaps obliged the State,
Nor paid a mere son's duty.

TIBURZIO
Even so.
Were you the son of Florence, yet endued
With all your present nobleness of soul,
No question, what I must communicate
Would not detach you from her.

LURIA
Me, detach?

TIBURZIO
Time urges. You will ruin presently
Pisa, you never knew, for Florence' sake
You think you know. I have from time to time
Made prize of certain secret missives sent
From Braccio here, the Commissary, home:
And knowing Florence otherwise, I piece
The entire chain out, from these its scattered links.
Your trial occupies the Signory;
They sit in judgment on your conduct now.
When men at home inquire into the acts
Which in the field e'en foes appreciate ...
Brief, they are Florentines! You, saving them,
Seek but the sure destruction saviors find.

LURIA
Tiburzio!

TIBURZIO
All the wonder is of course.
I am not here to teach you, nor direct,
Only to loyally apprise—scarce that.
This is the latest letter, sealed and safe,
As it left here an hour ago. One way

Of two thought free to Florence, I command.
The duplicate is on its road; but this,—
Read it, and then I shall have more to say.

LURIA
Florence!

TIBURZIO
Now, were yourself a Florentine,
This letter, let it hold the worst it can,
Would be no reason you should fall away.
The mother city is the mother still,
And recognition of the children's service
Her own affair; reward—there 's no reward!
But you are bound by quite another tie.
Nor nature shows, nor reason, why at first
A foreigner, born friend to all alike,
Should give himself to any special State
More than another, stand by Florence' side
Rather than Pisa; 't is as fair a city
You war against, as that you fight for—famed
As well as she in story, graced no less
With noble heads and patriotic hearts:
Nor to a stranger's eye would either cause,
Stripped of the cumulative loves and hates
Which take importance from familiar view,
Stand as the right and sole to be upheld.
Therefore, should the preponderating gift
Of love and trust, Florence was first to throw,
Which made you hers, not Pisa's, void the scale,—
Old ties dissolving, things resume their place,
And all begins again. Break seal and read!
At least let Pisa offer for you now!
And I, as a good Pisan, shall rejoice,
Though for myself I lose, in gaining you,
This last fight and its opportunity;
The chance it brings of saying Pisa yet,
Or in the turn of battle dying so
That shame should want its extreme bitterness.

LURIA
Tiburzio, you that fight for Pisa now
As I for Florence ... say my chance were yours!
You read this letter, and you find ... no, no!
Too mad!

TIBURZIO
I read the letter, find they purpose

When I have crushed their foe, to crush me: well?

LURIA
You, being their captain, what is it you do?

TIBURZIO
Why, as it is, all cities are alike;
As Florence pays you, Pisa will pay me.
I shall be as belied, whate'er the event,
As you, or more: my weak head, they will say
Prompted this last expedient, my faint heart
Entailed on them indelible disgrace,
Both which defects ask proper punishment.
Another tenure of obedience, mine!
You are no son of Pisa's: break and read!

LURIA
And act on what I read? What act were fit?
If the firm-fixed foundation of my faith
In Florence, who to me stands for mankind,
—If that break up and, disimprisoning
From the abyss ... Ah friend, it cannot be!
You may be very sage, yet—all the world
Having to fail, or your sagacity,
You do not wish to find yourself alone!
What would the world be worth? Whose love be sure?
The world remains: you are deceived!

TIBURZIO
Your hand!
I lead the vanguard.—If you fall, beside,
The better: I am left to speak! For me,
This was my duty, nor would I rejoice
If I could help, it misses its effect;
And after all you will look gallantly
Found dead here with that letter in your breast.

LURIA
Tiburzio—I would see these people once
And test them ere I answer finally!
At your arrival let the trumpet sound:
If mine return not then the wonted cry
It means that I believe—am Pisa's!

TIBURZIO
Well!

[Goes.

LURIA

My heart will have it he speaks true! My blood
Beats close to this Tiburzio as a friend.
If he had stept into my watch-tent, night
And the wild desert full of foes around,
I should have broke the bread and given the salt
Secure, and, when my hour of watch was done,
Taken my turn to sleep between his knees
Safe in the untroubled brow and honest cheek.
Oh world, where all things pass and naught abides,
Oh life, the long mutation—is it so?
Is it with life as with the body's change?
—Where, e'en though better follow, good must pass,
Nor manhood's strength can mate with boyhood's grace,
Nor age's wisdom, in its turn, find strength,
But silently the first gift dies away,
And though the new stays, never both at once.
Life's time of savage instinct o'er with me,
It fades and dies away, past trusting more,
As if to punish the ingratitude
With which I turned to grow in these new lights,
And learned to look with European eyes.
Yet it is better, this cold certain way,
Where Braccio's brow tells nothing, Puccio's mouth,
Domizia's eyes reject the searcher: yes!
For on their calm sagacity I lean,
Their sense of right, deliberate choice of good,
Sure, as they know my deeds, they deal with me.
Yes, that is better—that is best of all!
Such faith stays when mere wild belief would go.
Yes—when the desert creature's heart, at fault
Amid the scattering tempest's pillared sands,
Betrays its step into the pathless drift—
The calm instructed eye of man holds fast
By the sole bearing of the visible star,
Sure that when slow the whirling wreck subside,
The boundaries, lost now, shall be found again,—
The palm-trees and the pyramid over all.
Yes: I trust Florence: Pisa is deceived.

[Enter **BRACCIO**, **PUCCIO**, and **DOMIZIA**.

BRACCIO

Noon's at an end: no Lucca? You must fight.

LURIA

Do you remember ever, gentle friends,

I am no Florentine?

DOMIZIA
It is yourself
Who still are forcing us, importunately,
To bear in mind what else we should forget.

LURIA
For loss!—for what I lose in being none!
No shrewd man, such as you yourselves respect,
But would remind you of the stranger's loss
In natural friends and advocates at home,
Hereditary loves, even rivalships
With precedent for honor and reward.
Still, there's a gain, too! If you take it so,
The stranger's lot has special gain as well.
Do you forget there was my own far East
I might have given away myself to, once,
As now to Florence, and for such a gift,
Stood there like a descended deity?
There, worship waits us: what is it waits here?

[Shows the letter.

See! Chance has put into my hand the means
Of knowing what I earn, before I work.
Should I fight better, should I fight the worse,
With payment palpably before me? See!
Here lies my whole reward! Best learn it now
Or keep it for the end's entire delight?

BRACCIO
If you serve Florence as the vulgar serve,
For swordsman's-pay alone,—break seal and read!
In that case, you will find your full desert.

LURIA
Give me my one last happy moment, friends!
You need me now, and all the graciousness
This letter can contain will hardly balance
The after-feeling that you need no more.
This moment ... oh, the East has use with you!
Its sword still flashes—is not flung aside
With the past praise, in a dark corner yet!
How say you? 'Tis not so with Florentines—
Captains of yours: for them, the ended war
Is but a first step to the peace begun:
He who did well in war, just earns the right

To begin doing well in peace, you know:
And certain my precursors,—would not such
Look to themselves in such a chance as mine,
Secure the ground they trod upon, perhaps?
For I have heard, by fits, or seemed to hear,
Of strange mishap, mistake, ingratitude,
Treachery even. Say that one of you
Surmised this letter carried what might turn
To harm hereafter, cause him prejudice:
What would he do?

DOMIZIA [Hastily]
Thank God and take revenge!
Hurl her own force against the city straight!
And, even at the moment when the foe
Sounded defiance ...

[**TIBURZIO'S** trumpet sounds in the distance.

LURIA
Ah, you Florentines!
So would you do? Wisely for you, no doubt!
My simple Moorish instinct bids me clench
The obligation you relieve me from,
Still deeper!
[To **PUCCIO**] Sound our answer, I should say.
And thus:—

[Tearing the paper.

—The battle! That solves every doubt.

ACT III

AFTERNOON

PUCCIO, as making a report to **JACOPO**.

PUCCIO
And here, your captain must report the rest;
For, as I say, the main engagement over
And Luria's special part in it performed,
How could a subaltern like me expect
Leisure or leave to occupy the field
And glean what dropped from his wide harvesting?
I thought, when Lucca at the battle's end

Came up, just as the Pisan centre broke,
That Luria would detach me and prevent
The flying Pisans seeking what they found,
Friends in the rear, a point to rally by.
But no, more honorable proved my post!
I had the august captive to escort
Safe to our camp; some other could pursue,
Fight, and be famous; gentler chance was mine—
Tiburzio's wounded spirit must be soothed!
He's in the tent there.

JACOPO
Is the substance down?
I write—"The vanguard beaten and both wings
In full retreat, Tiburzio prisoner"—
And now,—" That they fell back and formed again
On Lucca's coming." Why then, after all,
'Tis half a victory, no conclusive one?

PUCCIO
Two operations where a sole had served.

JACOPO
And Luria's fault was—?

PUCCIO
Oh, for fault—not much!
He led the attack, a thought impetuously,
—There's commonly more prudence; now, he seemed
To hurry measures, otherwise well judged.
By over-concentrating strength at first
Against the enemy's van, both wings escaped:
That's reparable, yet it is a fault.

[Enter **BRACCIO**.

JACOPO
As good as a full victory to Florence,
With the advantage of a fault beside—
What is it, Puccio?—that by pressing forward
With too impetuous ...

BRACCIO
The report anon!
Thanks, sir—you have elsewhere a charge, I know.

[**PUCCIO** goes.

There's nothing done but I would do again;
Yet, Lapo, it may be the past proves nothing,
And Luria has kept faithful to the close.

JACOPO
I was for waiting.

BRACCIO
Yes: so was not I.
He could not choose but tear that letter—true!
Still, certain of his tones, I mind, and looks:—
You saw, too, with a fresher soul than I.
So, Porzio seemed an injured man, they say!
Well, I have gone upon the broad, sure ground.

[Enter **LURIA**, **PUCCIO**, and **DOMIZIA**.

LURIA [To **PUCCIO**]
Say, at his pleasure I will see Tiburzio!
All's at his pleasure.

DOMIZIA [To **LURIA**]
Were I not forewarned
You would reject, as you do constantly,
Praise,—I might tell you how you have deserved
Of Florence by this last and crowning feat:
But words offend.

LURIA
Nay, you may praise me now.
I want instruction every hour, I find,
On points where once I saw least need of it;
And praise, I have been used to slight perhaps,
Seems scarce so easily dispensed with now.
After a battle, half one's strength is gone;
The glorious passion in us once appeased,
Our reason's calm cold dreadful voice begins.
All justice, power and beauty scarce appear
Monopolized by Florence, as of late,
To me, the stranger: you, no doubt, may know
Why Pisa needs must bear her rival's yoke,
And peradventure I grow nearer you,
For I, too, want to know and be assured.
When a cause ceases to reward itself,
Its friend seeks fresh sustainments; praise in one,
And here stand you—you, lady, praise me well.
But yours—(your pardon)—is unlearnèd praise.
To the motive, the endeavor, the heart's self.

Your quick sense looks: you crown and call aright
The soul o' the purpose, ere 'tis shaped as act,
Takes flesh i' the world, and clothes itself a king.
But when the act comes, stands for what 'tis worth,
—Here's Puccio, the skilled soldier, he's my judge!
Was all well, Puccio?

PUCCIO
All was ... must be well:
If we beat Lucca presently, as doubtless ...
—No, there's no doubt, we must—all was well done.

LURIA
In truth? Still you are of the trade, my Puccio!
You have the fellow-craftsman's sympathy.
There's none cares, like a fellow of the craft,
For the all unestimated sum of pains
That go to a success the world can see:
They praise then, but the best they never know
—While you know! So, if envy mix with it,
Hate even, still the bottom-praise of all,
Whatever be the dregs, that drop's pure gold!
—For nothing's like it; nothing else records
Those daily, nightly drippings in the dark
Of the heart's blood, the world lets drop away
Forever—so, pure gold that praise must be!
And I have yours, my soldier! yet the best
Is still to come. There's one looks on apart
Whom all refers to, failure or success;
What's done might be our best, our utmost work,
And yet inadequate to serve his need.
Here's Braccio now, for Florence—here's our service—
Well done for us, seems it well done for him?
His chosen engine, tasked to its full strength
Answers the end? Should he have chosen higher?
Do we help Florence, now our best is wrought?

BRACCIO
This battle, with the foregone services,
Saves Florence.

LURIA
Why then, all is very well!
Here am I in the middle of my friends,
Who know me and who love me, one and all.
And yet ... 'tis like ... this instant while I speak
Is like the turning-moment of a dream
When ... Ah, you are not foreigners like me!

Well then, one always dreams of friends at home;
And always comes, I say, the turning-point
When something changes in the friendly eyes
That love and look on you ... so slight, so slight ...
And yet it tells you they are dead and gone,
Or changed and enemies, for all their words,
And all is mockery and a maddening show.
You now, so kind here, all you Florentines,
What is it in your eyes ... those lips, those brows ...
Nobody spoke it, yet I know it well!
Come now—this battle saves you, all's at end,
Your use of me is o'er, for good, for ill,—
Come now, what's done against me, while I speak,
In Florence? Come! I feel it in my blood,
My eyes, my hair, a voice is in my ears
That spite of all this smiling and soft speech
You are betraying me! What is it you do?
Have it your way, and think my use is over—
Think you are saved and may throw off the mask—
Have it my way, and think more work remains
Which I could do,—so, show you fear me not!
Or prudent be, or daring, as you choose,
But tell me—tell what I refused to know
At noon, lest heart should fail me! Well? That letter?
My fate is sealed at Florence! What is it?

BRACCIO
Sir, I shall not deny what you divine.
It is no novelty for innocence
To be suspected, but a privilege:
The after certain compensation comes.
Charges, I say not whether false or true,
Have been preferred against you some time since,
Which Florence was bound, plainly, to receive,
And which are therefore undergoing now
The due investigation. That is all.
I doubt not but your innocence will prove
Apparent and illustrious, as to me,
To them this evening, when the trial ends.

LURIA
My trial?

DOMIZIA
Florence, Florence to the end,
My whole heart thanks thee!

PUCCIO [To **BRACCIO**]

What is "trial," sir?
It was not for a trial,—surely, no—
I furnished you those notes from time to time?
I held myself aggrieved—I am a man—
And I might speak,—ay, and speak mere truth, too,
And yet not mean at bottom of my heart
What should assist a—trial, do you say?
You should have told me!

DOMIZIA
Nay, go on, go on!
His sentence! Do they sentence him? What is it?
The block—wheel?

BRACCIO
Sentence there is none as yet,
Nor shall I give my own opinion now
Of what it should be, or is like to be.
When it is passed, applaud or disapprove!
Up to that point, what is there to impugn?

LURIA
They are right, then, to try me?

BRACCIO
I assert,
Maintain and justify the absolute right
Of Florence to do all she can have done
In this procedure,—standing on her guard,
Receiving even services like yours
With utmost fit suspicious wariness.
In other matters, keep the mummery up!
Take all the experiences of all the world,
Each knowledge that broke through a heart to life,
Each reasoning which, to reach, burnt out a brain,
—In other cases, know these, warrant these,
And then dispense with these—'tis very well!
Let friend trust friend, and love demand love's like,
And gratitude be claimed for benefits,—
There's grace in that,—and when the fresh heart breaks,
The new brain proves a ruin, what of them?
Where is the matter of one moth the more
Singed in the candle, at a summer's end?
But Florence is no simple John or James
To have his toy, his fancy, his conceit
That he's the one excepted man by fate.
And, when fate shows him he's mistaken there,
Die with all good men's praise, and yield his place

To Paul and George intent to try their chance!
Florence exists because these pass away.
She's a contrivance to supply a type
Of man, which men's deficiencies refuse;
She binds so many, that she grows out of them—
Stands steady o'er their numbers, though they change
And pass away—there's always what upholds,
Always enough to fashion the great show.
As see, yon hanging city, in the sun,
Of shapely cloud substantially the same!
A thousand vapors rise and sink again,
Are interfused, and live their life and die,—
Yet ever hangs the steady show i' the air,
Under the sun's straight influence: that is well,
That is worth heaven should hold, and God should bless!
And so is Florence,—the unseen sun above,
Which draws and holds suspended all of us,
Binds transient vapors into a single cloud
Differing from each and better than they all.
And shall she dare to stake this permanence
On any one man's faith? Man's heart is weak,
And its temptations many: let her prove
Each servant to the very uttermost
Before she grant him her reward, I say!

DOMIZIA
And as for hearts she chances to mistake,
Wronged hearts, not destined to receive reward,
Though they deserve it, did she only know,
—What should she do for these?

BRACCIO
What does she not?
Say, that she gives them but herself to serve!
Here's Luria—what had profited his strength,
When half an hour of sober fancying
Had shown him step by step the uselessness
Of strength exerted for strength's proper sake?
But the truth is, she did create that strength,
Draw to the end the corresponding means.
The world is wide—are we the only men?
Oh, for the time, the social purpose' sake,
Use words agreed on, bandy epithets,
Call any man the sole great wise and good!
But shall we therefore, standing by ourselves,
Insult our souls and God with the same speech?
There, swarm the ignoble thousands under him:
What marks us from the hundreds and the tens?

Florence took up, turned all one way the soul
Of Luria with its fires, and here he glows!
She takes me out of all the world as him,
Fixing my coldness till like ice it checks
The fire! So, Braccio, Luria, which is best?

LURIA
Ah, brave me? And is this indeed the way
To gain your good word and sincere esteem?
Am I the baited animal that must turn
And fight his baiters to deserve their praise?
Obedience is mistake then? Be it so!
Do you indeed remember I stand here
The captain of the conquering army,—mine—
With all your tokens, praise and promise, ready
To show for what their names meant when you gave,
Not what you style them now you take away?
If I call in my troops to arbitrate,
And dash the first enthusiastic thrill
Of victory with this you menace now—
Commend to the instinctive popular sense,
My story first, your comment afterward,—
Will they take, think you, part with you or me?
If I say—I, the laborer they saw work,
Ending my work, ask pay, and find my lords
Have all this while provided silently
Against the day of pay and proving faith,
By what you call my sentence that's to come—
Will friends advise I wait complacently?
If I meet Florence half-way at their head,
What will you do, my mild antagonist?

BRACCIO
I will rise up like fire, proud and triumphant
That Florence knew you thoroughly and by me,
And so was saved. "See, Italy," I'll say,
"The crown of our precautions! Here's a man
Was far advanced, just touched on the belief
Less subtle cities had accorded long;
But we were wiser: at the end comes this!"
And from that minute, where is Luria? Lost!
The very stones of Florence cry against
The all-exacting, naught-enduring fool,
Who thus resents her first probation, flouts
As if he, only, shone and cast no shade,
He, only, walked the earth with privilege
Against suspicion, free where angels fear:
He, for the first inquisitive mother's-word,

Must turn, and stand on his defence, forsooth!
Reward? You will not be worth punishment!

LURIA

And Florence knew me thus! Thus I have lived,—
And thus you, with the clear fine intellect,
Braccio, the cold acute instructed mind,
Out of the stir, so calm and unconfused,
Reported me—how could you otherwise!
Ay?—and what dropped from you, just now, moreover?
Your information, Puccio?—Did your skill,
Your understanding sympathy approve
Such a report of me? Was this the end?
Or is even this the end? Can I stop here?
You, lady, with the woman's stand apart,
The heart to see with, past man's brain and eyes,
... I cannot fathom why you should destroy
The unoffending one, you call your friend—
Still, lessoned by the good examples here
Of friendship, 'tis but natural I ask—
Had you a further aim, in aught you urged,
Than your friend's profit—in all those instances
Of perfidy, all Florence wrought of wrong—
All I remember now for the first time?

DOMIZIA

I am a daughter of the Traversari,
Sister of Porzio and of Berto both,
So, have foreseen all that has come to pass.
I knew the Florence that could doubt their faith,
Must needs mistrust a stranger's—dealing them
Punishment, would deny him his reward.
And I believed, the shame they bore and died,
He would not bear, but live and fight against—
Seeing he was of other stuff than they.

LURIA

Hear them! All these against one foreigner!
And all this while, where is, in the whole world,
To his good faith a single witness?

TIBURZIO [Who has entered unseen during the preceding dialogue]
Here!
Thus I bear witness, not in word but deed.
I live for Pisa; she's not lost to-day
By many chances—much prevents from that!
Her army has been beaten, I am here,
But Lucca comes at last, one happy chance!

I rather would see Pisa three times lost
Than saved by any traitor, even by you;
The example of a traitor's happy fortune
Would bring more evil in the end than good;—
Pisa rejects the traitor, craves yourself!
I, in her name, resign forthwith to you
My charge,—the highest office, sword and shield!
You shall not, by my counsel, turn on Florence
Your army, give her calumny that ground—
Nor bring one soldier: be you all we gain!
And all she'll lose,—a head to deck some bridge,
And save the cost o' the crown should deck the head.
Leave her to perish in her perfidy,
Plague-stricken and stripped naked to all eyes,
A proverb and a by-word in all mouths!
Go you to Pisa! Florence is my place—
Leave me to tell her of the rectitude,
I, from the first, told Pisa, knowing it.
To Pisa!

DOMIZIA
Ah my Braccio, are you caught?

BRACCIO
Puccio, good soldier and good citizen,
Whom I have ever kept beneath my eye,
Ready as fit, to serve in this event
Florence, who clear foretold it from the first—
Through me, she gives you the command and charge
She takes, through me, from him who held it late!
A painful trial, very sore, was yours:
All that could draw out, marshal in array
The selfish passions 'gainst the public good—
Slights, scorns, neglects, were heaped on you to hear:
And ever you did bear and bow the head!
It had been sorry trial, to precede
Your feet, hold up the promise of reward
For luring gleam; your footsteps kept the track
Through dark and doubt: take all the light at once!
Trial is over, consummation shines;
Well have you served, as well henceforth command!

PUCCIO
No, no ... I dare not! I am grateful, glad;
But Luria—you shall understand he's wronged:
And he's my captain—this is not the way
We soldiers climb to fortune: think again!
The sentence is not even passed, beside!

I dare not: where's the soldier could?

LURIA
Now, Florence—
Is it to be? You will know all the strength
O' the savage—to your neck the proof must go?
You will prove the brute nature? Ah, I see!
The savage plainly is impassible—
He keeps his calm way through insulting words,
Sarcastic looks, sharp gestures—one of which
Would stop you, fatal to your finer sense,
But if he stolidly advance, march mute
Without a mark upon his callous hide,
Through the mere brushwood you grow angry with,
And leave the tatters of your flesh upon,
—You have to learn that when the true bar comes,
The murk mid-forest, the grand obstacle,
Which when you reach, you give the labor up,
Nor dash on, but lie down composed before,
—He goes against it, like the brute he is:
It falls before him, or he dies in his course.
I kept my course through past ingratitude:
I saw—it does seem, now, as if I saw,
Could not but see, those insults as they fell,
—Ay, let them glance from off me, very like,
Laughing, perhaps, to think the quality
You grew so bold on, while you so despised
The Moor's dull mute inapprehensive mood,
Was saving you: I bore and kept my course.
Now real wrong fronts me: see if I succumb!
Florence withstands me? I will punish her.

At night my sentence will arrive, you say.
Till then I cannot, if I would, rebel
—Unauthorized to lay my office down,
Retaining my full power to will and do:
After—it is to see. Tiburzio, thanks!
Go; you are free: join Lucca! I suspend
All further operations till to-night.
Thank you, and for the silence most of all!
[To **BRACCIO**] Let my complacent bland accuser go
Carry his self-approving head and heart
Safe through the army which would trample him
Dead in a moment at my word or sign!
Go, sir, to Florence; tell friends what I say—
That while I wait my sentence, theirs waits them!
[To **DOMIZIA**] You, lady,—you have black Italian eyes!
I would be generous if I might: oh, yes—

For I remember how so oft you seemed
Inclined at heart to break the barrier down
Which Florence finds God built between us both.
Alas, for generosity! this hour
Asks retribution: bear it as you may,
I must—the Moor—the savage,—pardon you!
Puccio, my trusty soldier, see them forth!

ACT IV

EVENING

Enter **PUCCIO** and **JACOPO**.

PUCCIO
What Luria will do? Ah, 'tis yours, fair sir,
Your and your subtle-witted master's part,
To tell me that; I tell you what he can.

JACOPO
Friend, you mistake my station: I observe
The game, watch how my betters play, no more.

PUCCIO
But mankind are not pieces—there's your fault!
You cannot push them, and, the first move made,
Lean back and study what the next shall be,
In confidence that, when 'tis fixed upon,
You find just where you left them, blacks and whites:
Men go on moving when your hand's away.
You build, I notice, firm on Luria's faith
This whole time,—firmlier than I choose to build,
Who never doubted it—of old, that is—
With Luria in his ordinary mind.
But now, oppression makes the wise man mad:
How do I know he will not turn and stand
And hold his own against you, as he may?
Suppose he but withdraw to Pisa—well,—
Then, even if all happen to your wish,
Which is a chance ...

JACOPO
Nay—'twas an oversight,
Not waiting till the proper warrant came:
You could not take what was not ours to give.
But when at night the sentence really comes,

Our city authorizes past dispute
Luria's removal and transfers the charge,
You will perceive your duty and accept?

PUCCIO

Accept what? muster-rolls of soldiers' names?
An army upon paper? I want men,
The hearts as well as hands—and where's a heart
But beats with Luria, in the multitude
I come from walking through by Luria's side?
You gave them Luria, set him thus to grow,
Head-like, upon their trunk; one heart feeds both,
They feel him there, live twice, and well know why.
—For they do know, if you are ignorant,
Who kept his own place and respected theirs,
Managed their sweat, yet never spared his blood.
All was your act: another might have served—
There's peradventure no such dearth of heads—
But you chose Luria: so, they grew one flesh,
And now, for nothing they can understand,
Luria removed, off is to roll the head;
The body's mine—much I shall do with it!

JACOPO

That's at the worst.

PUCCIO

No—at the best, it is!
Best, do you hear? I saw them by his side.
Only we two with Luria in the camp
Are left that keep the secret? You think that?
Hear what I know: from rear to van, no heart
But felt the quiet patient hero there
Was wronged, nor in the moveless ranks an eye
But glancing told its fellow the whole story
Of that convicted silent knot of spies
Who passed through them to Florence; they might pass—
No breast but gladlier beat when free of such!
Our troops will catch up Luria, close him round,
Bear him to Florence as their natural lord,
Partake his fortune, live or die with him.

JACOPO

And by mistake catch up along with him
Puccio, no doubt, compelled in self despite
To still continue second in command!

PUCCIO

No, sir, no second nor so fortunate!
Your tricks succeed with me too well for that!
I am as you have made me, live and die
To serve your end—a mere trained fighting-hack,
With words, you laugh at while they leave your mouth,
For my life's rule and ordinance of God!
I have to do my duty, keep my faith,
And earn my praise, and guard against my blame,
As I was trained. I shall accept your charge,
And fight against one better than myself,
Spite of my heart's conviction of his worth—
That, you may count on!—just as hitherto
I have gone on, persuaded I was wronged,
Slighted, insulted, terms we learn by rote,—
All because Luria superseded me—
Because the better nature, fresh-inspired,
Mounted above me to its proper place!
What mattered all the kindly graciousness,
The cordial brother's-bearing? This was clear—
I, once the captain, now was subaltern,
And so must keep complaining like a fool!
Go, take the curse of a lost soul, I say!
You neither play your puppets to the end,
Nor treat the real man,—for his realness' sake
Thrust rudely in their place,—with such regard
As might console them for their altered rank.
Me, the mere steady soldier, you depose
For Luria, and here's all your pet deserves!
Of what account, then, is your laughing-stock?
One word for all: whatever Luria does,
—If backed by his indignant troops he turn,
Revenge himself, and Florence go to ground,—
Or, for a signal everlasting shame,
He pardon you, simply seek better friends,
Side with the Pisans and Lucchese for change
—And if I, pledged to ingrates past belief,
Dare fight against a man such fools call false,
Who, inasmuch as he was true, fights me,—
Whichever way he win, he wins for worth,
For every soldier, for all true and good!
Sir, chronicling the rest, omit not this!

[As they go, enter **LURIA** and **HUSAIN**.

HUSAIN
Saw'st thou?—For they are gone! The world lies bare
Before thee, to be tasted, felt and seen
Like what it is, now Florence goes away!

Thou livest now, with men art man again!
Those Florentines were all to thee of old;
But Braccio, but Domizia, gone is each,
There lie beneath thee thine own multitudes!
Saw'st thou?

LURIA
I saw.

HUSAIN
Then, hold thy course, my king!
The years return. Let thy heart have its way:
Ah, they would play with thee as with all else,
Turn thee to use, and fashion thee anew,
Find out God's fault in thee as in the rest?
Oh watch, oh listen only to these fiends
Once at their occupation! Ere we know,
The free great heaven is shut, their stifling pall
Drops till it frets the very tingling hair,
So weighs it on our head,—and, for the earth,
Our common earth is tethered up and down,
Over and across—"here shalt thou move," they cry!

LURIA
Ay, Husain?

HUSAIN
So have they spoiled all beside!
So stands a man girt round with Florentines,
Priests, graybeards, Braccios, women, boys and spies,
All in one tale, all singing the same song,
How thou must house, and live at bed and board,
Take pledge and give it, go their every way,
Breathe to their measure, make thy blood beat time
With theirs—- or, all is nothing—thou art lost—
A savage, how shouldst thou perceive as they?
Feel glad to stand 'neath God's close naked hand!
Look up to it! Why, down they pull thy neck,
Lest it crush thee, who feel'st it and wouldst kiss,
Without their priests that needs must glove it first,
Lest peradventure flesh offend thy lip.
Love woman! Why, a very beast thou art!
Thou must ...

LURIA
Peace, Husain!

HUSAIN

Ay, but, spoiling all,
For all, else true things, substituting false,
That they should dare spoil, of all instincts, thine!
Should dare to take thee with thine instincts up,
Thy battle-ardors, like a ball of fire,
And class them and allow them place and play
So far, no farther—unabashed the while!
Thou with the soul that never can take rest—
Thou born to do, undo, and do again,
And never to be still,—wouldst thou make war?
Oh, that is commendable, just and right!
"Come over," say they, "have the honor due
In living out thy nature! Fight thy best:
It is to be for Florence, not thyself!
For thee, it were a horror and a plague;
For us, when war is made for Florence, see,
How all is changed: the fire that fed on earth
Now towers to heaven!"—

LURIA
And what sealed up so long
My Husain's mouth?

HUSAIN
Oh friend, oh lord—for me,
What am I?—I was silent at thy side,
Who am a part of thee. It is thy hand,
Thy foot that glows when in the heart fresh blood
Boils up, thou heart of me! Now, live again,
Again love as thou likest, hate as free!
Turn to no Braccios nor Domizias now,
To ask, before thy very limbs dare move,
If Florence' welfare be concerned thereby!

LURIA
So clear what Florence must expect of me?

HUSAIN
Both armies against Florence! Take revenge!
Wide, deep—to live upon, in feeling now,—
And, after live, in memory, year by year—
And, with the dear conviction, die at last!
She lies now at thy pleasure: pleasure have!
Their vaunted intellect that gilds our sense,
And blends with life, to show it better by,
—How think'st thou?—I have turned that light on them!
They called our thirst of war a transient thing;
"The battle-element must pass away

From life," they said, "and leave a tranquil world."
—Master, I took their light and turned it full
On that dull turgid vein they said would burst
And pass away; and as I looked on life,
Still everywhere I tracked this, though it hid
And shifted, lay so silent as it thought,
Changed shape and hue yet ever was the same.
Why, 't was all fighting, all their nobler life!
All work was fighting, every harm—defeat,
And every joy obtained—a victory!
Be not their dupe!
—Their dupe? That hour is past!
Here stand'st thou in the glory and the calm:
All is determined. Silence for me now!

[**HUSAIN** goes.

LURIA
Have I heard all?

DOMIZIA [Advancing from the background]
No, Luria, I remain!
Not from the motives these have urged on thee,
Ignoble, insufficient, incomplete,
And pregnant each with sure seeds of decay,
As failing of sustainment from thyself,
—Neither from low revenge, nor selfishness,
Nor savage lust of power, nor one, nor all,
Shalt thou abolish Florence! I proclaim
The angel in thee, and reject the sprites
Which ineffectual crowd about his strength,
And mingle with his work and claim a share!
Inconsciously to the augustest end
Thou hast arisen: second not in rank
So much as time, to him who first ordained
That Florence, thou art to destroy, should be.
Yet him a star, too, guided, who broke first
The pride of lonely power, the life apart,
And made the eminences, each to each,
Lean o'er the level world and let it lie
Safe from the thunder henceforth 'neath their tops;
So the few famous men of old combined,
And let the multitude rise underneath,
And reach them and unite—so Florence grew:
Braccio speaks true, it was well worth the price.
But when the sheltered many grew in pride
And grudged the station of the elected ones,
Who, greater than their kind, are truly great

Only in voluntary servitude—
Time was for thee to rise, and thou art here.
Such plague possessed this Florence: who can tell
The mighty girth and greatness at the heart
Of those so perfect pillars of the grove
She pulled down in her envy? Who as I,
The light weak parasite born but to twine
Round each of them and, measuring them, live?
My light love keeps the matchless circle safe,
My slender life proves what has passed away.
I lived when they departed; lived to cling
To thee, the mighty stranger; thou wouldst rise
And burst the thraldom, and avenge, I knew.
I have done nothing; all was thy strong bole.
But a bird's weight can break the infant tree
Which after holds an aery in its arms,
And 't was my care that naught should warp thy spire
From rising to the height; the roof is reached
O' the forest, break through, see extend the sky!
Go on to Florence, Luria! 'T is man's cause!
Fail thou, and thine own fall were least to dread:
Thou keepest Florence in her evil way,
Encouragest her sin so much the more—
And while the ignoble past is justified,
Thou all the surelier warp'st the future growth,
The chiefs to come, the Lurias yet unborn,
That, greater than thyself, are reached o'er thee
Who giv'st the vantage-ground their foes require,
As o'er my prostrate House thyself wast reached!
Man calls thee, God requites thee! All is said,
The mission of my House fulfilled at last:
And the mere woman, speaking for herself,
Reserves speech—it is now no woman's time.

[DOMIZIA goes.

LURIA
Thus at the last must figure Luria, then!
Doing the various work of all his friends,
And answering every purpose save his own.
No doubt, 't is well for them to wish; but him—
After the exploit what were left? Perchance
A little pride upon the swarthy brow,
At having brought successfully to bear
'Gainst Florence' self her own especial arms,—
Her craftiness, impelled by fiercer strength
From Moorish blood than feeds the northern wit.
But after!—once the easy vengeance willed,

Beautiful Florence at a word laid low
—(Not in her domes and towers and palaces,
Not even in a dream, that outrage!)—low,
As shamed in her own eyes henceforth forever,
Low, for the rival cities round to laugh,
Conquered and pardoned by a hireling Moor!
—For him, who did the irreparable wrong,
What would be left, his life's illusion fled,—
What hope or trust in the forlorn wide world?
How strange that Florence should mistake me so!
Whence grew this? What withdrew her faith from me?
Some cause! These fretful-blooded children talk
Against their mother,—they are wronged, they say—
Notable wrongs her smile makes up again!
So, taking fire at each supposed offence,
They may speak rashly, suffer for their speech:
But what could it have been in word or deed
Thus injured me? Some one word spoken more
Out of my heart, and all had changed perhaps.
My fault, it must have been,—for, what gain they?
Why risk the danger? See, what I could do!
And my fault, wherefore visit upon them,
My Florentines? The notable revenge
I meditated! To stay passively.
Attend their summons, be as they dispose!
Why, if my very soldiers keep the rank,
And if my chieftains acquiesce, what then?
I ruin Florence, teach her friends mistrust,
Confirm her enemies in harsh belief,
And when she finds one day, as find she must,
The strange mistake, and how my heart was hers,
Shall it console me, that my Florentines
Walk with a sadder step, in graver guise,
Who took me with such frankness, praised me so,
At the glad outset? Had they loved me less,
They had less feared what seemed a change in me.
And after all, who did the harm? Not they!
How could they interpose with those old fools
I' the council? Suffer for those old fools' sake—
They, who made pictures of me, sang the songs
About my battles? Ah, we Moors get blind
Out of our proper world, where we can see!
The sun that guides is closer to us! There—
There, my own orb! He sinks from out the sky!
Why, there! a whole day has he blessed the land,
My land, our Florence all about the hills,
The fields and gardens, vineyards, olive-grounds,
All have been blest—and yet we Florentines,

With souls intent upon our battle here,
Found that he rose too soon, or set too late,
Gave us no vantage, or gave Pisa much—
Therefore we wronged him! Does he turn in ire
To burn the earth that cannot understand?
Or drop out quietly, and leave the sky,
His task once ended? Night wipes blame away.
Another morning from my East shall spring
And find all eyes at leisure, all disposed
To watch and understand its work, no doubt.
So, praise the new sun, the successor praise,
Praise the new Luria and forget the old!

[Taking a phial from his breast.

—Strange! This is all I brought from my own land
To help me: Europe would supply the rest,
All needs beside, all other helps save one!
I thought of adverse fortune, battle lost,
The natural upbraiding of the loser,
And then this quiet remedy to seek
At end of the disastrous day.

[He drinks.

'T is sought!
This was my happy triumph-morning: Florence
Is saved: I drink this, and ere night,—die! Strange!

ACT V

NIGHT

LURIA and **PUCCIO**

LURIA
I thought to do this, not to talk this: well,
Such were my projects for the city's good,
To help her in attack or by defence.
Time, here as elsewhere, soon or late may take
Our foresight by surprise through chance and change;
But not a little we provide against
—If you see clear on every point.

PUCCIO
Most clear.

LURIA

Then all is said—not much, if you count words,
Yet to an understanding ear enough;
And all that my brief stay permits, beside.
Nor must you blame me, as I sought to teach
My elder in command, or threw a doubt
Upon the very skill, it comforts me
To know I leave,—your steady soldiership
Which never failed me: yet, because it seemed
A stranger's eye might haply note defect
That skill, through use and custom, over-looks—
I have gone into the old cares once more,
As if I had to come and save again
Florence—that May—that morning! 'T is night now.
Well—I broke off with?...

PUCCIO

Of the past campaign
You spoke—of measures to be kept in mind
For future use.

LURIA

True, so ... but, time—no time!
As well end here: remember this, and me!
Farewell now!

PUCCIO

Dare I speak?

LURIA

South o' the river—
How is the second stream called ... no,—the third?

PUCCIO

Pesa.

LURIA

And a stone's-cast from the fording-place,
To the east,—the little mount's name?

PUCCIO

Lupo.

LURIA

Ay!
Ay—there the tower, and all that side is safe!
With San Romano, west of Evola,

San Miniato, Scala, Empoli,
Five towers in all,—forget not!

PUCCIO
Fear not me!

LURIA
—Nor to memorialize the Council now,
I' the easy hour, on those battalions' claim,
Who forced a pass by Staggia on the hills,
And kept the Sienese at check!

PUCCIO
One word—
Sir, I must speak! That you submit yourself
To Florence' bidding, howsoe'er it prove,
And give up the command to me—is much,
Too much, perhaps: but what you tell me now,
Even will affect the other course you choose—
Poor as it may be, perils even that!
Refuge you seek at Pisa: yet these plans
All militate for Florence, all conclude
Your formidable work to make her queen
O' the country,—which her rivals rose against
When you began it,—which to interrupt,
Pisa would buy you off at any price!
You cannot mean to sue for Pisa's help,
With this made perfect and on record?

LURIA
I—
At Pisa, and for refuge, do you say?

PUCCIO
Where are you going, then? You must decide
On leaving us, a silent fugitive,
Alone, at night—you, stealing through our lines,
Who were this morning's Luria,—you escape
To painfully begin the world once more,
With such a past, as it had never been!
Where are you going?

LURIA
Not so far, my Puccio,
But that I hope to hear, enjoy and praise
(If you mind praise from your old captain yet)
Each happy blow you strike for Florence!

PUCCIO
Ay,
But ere you gain your shelter, what may come?
For see—though nothing 's surely known as yet,
Still—truth must out—I apprehend the worst.
If mere suspicion stood for certainty
Before, there 's nothing can arrest the step
Of Florence toward your ruin, once on foot.
Forgive her fifty times, it matters not!
And having disbelieved your innocence,
How can she trust your magnanimity?
You may do harm to her—why then, you will!
And Florence is sagacious in pursuit.
Have you a friend to count on?

LURIA
One sure friend.

PUCCIO
Potent?

LURIA
All-potent.

PUCCIO
And he is apprised?

LURIA
He waits me.

PUCCIO
So!—Then I, put in your place,
Making my profit of all done by you,
Calling your labors mine, reaping their fruit,
To this, the State's gift, now add yours beside—
That I may take as my peculiar store
These your instructions to work Florence good.
And if, by putting some few happily
In practice, I should both advantage her
And draw down honor on myself,—what then?

LURIA
Do it, my Puccio! I shall know and praise!

PUCCIO
Though so, men say, "mark what we gain by change
—A Puccio for a Luria!"

LURIA
Even so!

PUCCIO
Then, not for fifty hundred Florences
Would I accept one office save my own,
Fill any other than my rightful post
Here at your feet, my captain and my lord!
That such a cloud should break, such trouble be,
Ere a man settle, soul and body, down
Into his true place and take rest forever!
Here were my wise eyes fixed on your right hand,
And so the bad thoughts came and the worse words,
And all went wrong and painfully enough,—
No wonder,—till, the right spot stumbled on,
All the jar stops, and there is peace at once!
I am yours now,—a tool your right hand wields!
God's love, that I should live, the man I am,
On orders, warrants, patents and the like,
As if there were no glowing eye i' the world
To glance straight inspiration to my brain,
No glorious heart to give mine twice the beats!
For, see—my doubt, where is it?—fear? 't is flown!
And Florence and her anger are a tale
To scare a child! Why, half-a-dozen words
Will tell her, spoken as I now can speak,
Her error, my past folly—and all 's right,
And you are Luria, our great chief again!
Or at the worst—which worst were best of all—
To exile or to death I follow you!

LURIA
Thanks, Puccio! Let me use the privilege
You grant me: if I still command you,—stay!
Remain here, my vicegerent, it shall be,
And not successor: let me, as of old,
Still serve the State, my spirit prompting yours—
Still triumph, one for both. There! Leave me now!
You cannot disobey my first command?
Remember what I spoke of Jacopo,
And what you promised to concert with him!
Send him to speak with me—nay, no farewell!
You shall be by me when the sentence comes.

[**PUCCIO** goes.

So, there 's one Florentine returns again!
Out of the genial morning company.

One face is left to take into the night

[Enter **JACOPO**.

JACOPO
I wait for your command, sir.

LURIA
What, so soon?
I thank your ready presence and fair word.
I used to notice you in early days
As of the other species, so to speak,
Those watchers of the lives of us who act—
That weigh our motives, scrutinize our thoughts.
So, I propound this to your faculty
As you would tell me, were a town to take
... That is, of old. I am departing hence
Under these imputations; that is naught—
I leave no friend on whom they may rebound,
Hardly a name behind me in the land,
Being a stranger: all the more behooves
That I regard how altered were the case
With natives of the country, Florentines
On whom the like mischance should fall: the roots
O' the tree survive the ruin of the trunk—
No root of mine will throb, you understand.
But I had predecessors, Florentines,
Accused as I am now, and punished so—
The Traversari: you know more than I
How stigmatized they are and lost in shame.
Now Puccio, who succeeds me in command,
Both served them and succeeded, in due time;
He knows the way, holds proper documents,
And has the power to lay the simple truth
Before an active spirit, as I count yours:
And also there 's Tiburzio, my new friend,
Will, at a word, confirm such evidence,
He being the great chivalric soul we know.
I put it to your tact, sir—were 't not well,
—A grace, though but for contrast's sake, no more,—
If you who witness, and have borne a share
Involuntarily in my mischance,
Should, of your proper motion, set your skill
To indicate—that is, investigate
The right or wrong of what mischance befell
Those famous citizens, your countrymen?
Nay, you shall promise nothing: but reflect,
And if your sense of justice prompt you—good!

JACOPO

And if, the trial past, their fame stand clear
To all men's eyes, as yours, my lord, to mine—
Their ghosts may sleep in quiet satisfied!
For me, a straw thrown up into the air,
My testimony goes for a straw's worth.
I used to hold by the instructed brain,
And move with Braccio as my master-wind;
The heart leads surelier: I must move with you—
As greatest now, who ever were the best.
So, let the last and humblest of your servants
Accept your charge, as Braccio's heretofore,
And tender homage by obeying you!

[JACOPO goes.

LURIA

Another!—Luria goes not poorly forth.
If we could wait! The only fault 's with time;
All men become good creatures: but so slow!

[Enter **DOMIZIA**.

LURIA

Ah, you once more?

DOMIZIA

Domizia, whom you knew,
Performed her task, and died with it. 'T is I,
Another woman, you have never known.
Let the past sleep now!

LURIA

I have done with it.

DOMIZIA

How inexhaustibly the spirit grows!
One object, she seemed erewhile born to reach
With her whole energies and die content,—
So like a wall at the world's edge it stood,
With naught beyond to live for,—is that reached?—
Already are new undreamed energies
Outgrowing under, and extending farther
To a new object; there 's another world.
See! I have told the purpose of my life;
'T is gained: you are decided, well or ill—
You march on Florence, or submit to her—

My work is done with you, your brow declares.
But—leave you?—More of you seems yet to reach:
I stay for what I just begin to see.

LURIA

So that you turn not to the past!

DOMIZIA

You trace
Nothing but ill in it—my selfish impulse,
Which sought its end and disregarded yours?

LURIA

Speak not against your nature: best, each keep
His own—you, yours—most, now that I keep mine,
—At least, fall by it, having too weakly stood.
God's finger marks distinctions, all so fine,
We would confound: the lesser has its use,
Which, when it apes the greater, is foregone.
I, born a Moor, lived half a Florentine;
But, punished properly, can end, a Moor.
Beside, there's something makes me understand
Your nature: I have seen it.

DOMIZIA

Aught like mine?

LURIA

In my own East ... if you would stoop and help
My barbarous illustration! It sounds ill;
Yet there's no wrong at bottom: rather, praise.

DOMIZIA

Well?

LURIA

We have creatures there, which if you saw
The first time, you would doubtless marvel at
For their surpassing beauty, craft and strength.
And though it were a lively moment's shock
When you first found the purpose of forked tongues
That seem innocuous in their lambent play,
Yet, once made know such grace requires such guard,
Your reason soon would acquiesce, I think,
In wisdom which made all things for the best—
So, take them, good with ill, contentedly,
The prominent beauty with the latent sting,
I am glad to have seen you wondrous Florentines:

Yet ...

DOMIZIA
I am here to listen.

LURIA
My own East!
How nearer God we were! He glows above
With scarce an intervention, presses close
And palpitatingly, his soul o'er ours:
We feel him, nor by painful reason know!
The everlasting minute of creation
Is felt there; now it is, as it was then;
All changes at his instantaneous will,
Not by the operation of a law
Whose maker is elsewhere at other work.
His hand is still engaged upon his world—
Man's praise can forward it, man's prayer suspend,
For is not God all-mighty? To recast
The world, erase old things and make them new,
What costs it Him? So, man breathes nobly there.
And inasmuch as feeling, the East's gift,
Is quick and transient—comes, and lo, is gone—
While Northern thought is slow and durable,
Surely a mission was reserved for me,
Who, born with a perception of the power
And use of the North's thought for us of the East,
Should have remained, turned knowledge to account,
Giving thought's character and permanence
To the too transitory feeling there—
Writing God's message plain in mortal words.
Instead of which, I leave my fated field
For this where such a task is needed least,
Where all are born consummate in the art
I just perceive a chance of making mine,—
And then, deserting thus my early post,
I wonder that the men I come among
Mistake me! There, how all had understood,
Still brought fresh stuff for me to stamp and keep,
Fresh instinct to translate them into law!
Me, who ...

DOMIZIA
Who here the greater task achieve,
More needful even: who have brought fresh stuff
For us to mould, interpret and prove right,—
New feeling fresh from God, which, could we know
O' the instant, where had been our need of it?

—Whose life re-teaches us what life should be,
What faith is, loyalty and simpleness,
All, once revealed but taught us so long since
That, having mere tradition of the fact,—
Truth copied falteringly from copies faint,
The early traits all dropped away,—we said
On sight of faith like yours, "So looks not faith
We understand, described and praised before."
But still, the feat was dared; and though at first
It suffered from our haste, yet trace by trace
Old memories reappear, old truth returns,
Our slow thought does its work, and all's reknown.
Oh noble Luria! What you have decreed
I see not, but no animal revenge.
No brute-like punishment of bad by worse—
It cannot be, the gross and vulgar way
Traced for me by convention and mistake,
Has gained that calm approving eye and brow!
Spare Florence, after all! Let Luria trust
To his own soul, he whom I trust with mine!

LURIA
In time!

DOMIZIA
How, Luria?

LURIA
It is midnight now,
And they arrive from Florence with my fate.

DOMIZIA
I hear no step.

LURIA
I feel one, as you say.

[Enter **HUSAIN**.

HUSAIN
The man returned from Florence!

LURIA
As I knew.

HUSAIN
He seeks thee.

LURIA
And I only wait for him.
Aught else?

HUSAIN
A movement of the Lucchese troops
Southward—

LURIA
Toward Florence? Have out instantly ...
Ah, old use clings! Puccio must care henceforth.
In—quick—'tis nearly midnight! Bid him come!

[Enter **TIBURZIO, BRACCIO,** and **PUCCIO.**

LURIA
Tiburzio?—not at Pisa?

TIBURZIO
I return
From Florence: I serve Pisa, and must think
By such procedure I have served her best.
A people is but the attempt of many
To rise to the completer life of one;
And those who live as models for the mass
Are singly of more value than they all.
Such man are you, and such a time is this,
That your sole fate concerns a nation more
Than much apparent welfare: that to prove
Your rectitude, and duly crown the same,
Imports us far beyond to-day's event,
A battle's loss or gain: man's mass remains,—
Keep but God's model safe, new men will rise
To take its mould, and other days to prove
How great a good was Luria's glory. True—
I might go try my fortune as you urged,
And, joining Lucca, helped by your disgrace,
Repair our harm—so were to-day's work done;
But where leave Luria for our sons to see?
No, I look farther. I have testified
(Declaring my submission to your arms)
Her full success to Florence, making clear
Your probity, as none else could: I spoke,
And out it shone!

LURIA
Ah—until Braccio spoke!

BRACCIO
Till Braccio told in just a word the whole—
His lapse to error, his return to knowledge:
Which told ... Nay, Luria, I should droop the head,
I whom shame rests with! Yet I dare look up,
Sure of your pardon how I sue for it,
Knowing you wholly. Let the midnight end!
'Tis morn approaches! Still you answer not?
Sunshine succeeds the shadow passed away;
Our faces, which phantasmal grew and false,
Are all that felt it: they change round you, turn
Truly themselves now in its vanishing.
Speak, Luria! Here begins your true career:
Look up, advance! All now is possible,
Fact's grandeur, no false dreaming! Dare and do!
And every prophecy shall be fulfilled
Save one—(nay, now your word must come at last)
—That you would punish Florence!

HUSAIN [Pointing to **LURIA'S** dead body]
That is done.

Robert Browning – A Short Biography

He is the equal of any Victorian Poet that could be mentioned. However, Browning continues to be in the shadow of Tennyson, Arnold, Hopkins, Morris and many others.

Robert Browning was born on May 7th, 1812 in Walworth in the parish of Camberwell, London. He was baptized on June 14th, 1812, at Lock's Fields Independent Chapel, York Street, Walworth.

Browning's early years were certainly very interesting. His mother was an excellent pianist and a very devout evangelical Christian. His father, who worked as a clerk at the Bank of England, was also an artist, scholar, antiquarian, and collector of books and pictures. Indeed, he amassed more than 6,000 volumes of rare books including works in Greek, Hebrew, Latin, French, Italian, and Spanish. For the young and curious Browning, it was a wonderful resource, added to which his father was a guiding force in his education.

Many accounts attest that Browning was already proficient at reading and writing by the age of five. He is said to have been a bright but anxious student and to have studied and learnt Latin, Greek, and French by the time he was fourteen. From fourteen to sixteen he was educated at home, tutored in music, drawing, dancing, and horsemanship. Certainly, language and the arts were two areas the young Browning both absorbed and pushed himself towards.

At the age of twelve he wrote a volume of Byronic verse he called Incondita, which his parents attempted to have published. The attempts were unsuccessful and, disappointed, Browning destroyed the work.

In 1825, a cousin gave Browning a collection of Percy Bysshe Shelley's poetry; Browning was so enamored with the poems that he asked for the rest of Shelley's works for his thirteenth birthday. In fact, Browning then went the extra mile, declaring himself to be both a vegetarian and an atheist in honour of his hero.

Intriguingly it seems that the rejection of his first volume didn't dim his appreciation of other poets, but it appears to have stopped him writing any poems between the ages of thirteen and twenty.

In 1828, Browning enrolled at the newly-opened University of London. He was uncomfortable with the experience and he soon left, anxious to read and absorb at his own pace.

His education which, overall is notably rambling and lacks a structure that many of his artistic contemporaries enjoyed, i.e. excellent public schooling and then a degree at Oxford or Cambridge, may present many of his critics with ammunition to criticize, but alternatively his hap-hazard education certainly contributed to many of the references that baffled both critics and his audience, but they tellingly show the breath and scale of what he could turn words too. What others would call obscure references were, to Browning, remarkably obvious.

Browning's early career was very promising. His long poem Pauline (of which only a fragment was ever finished and published) brought him to the attention of the Pre-Raphaelite master Dante Gabriel Rossetti and his difficult Paracelsus (published in 1835) was warmly admired by both Dickens and Wordsworth.

In the 1830s he met the actor William Macready and was encouraged to develop and turn his talents to the stage by writing verse drama. But these plays, including Strafford, which ran for five nights in 1837, and those contained within the Bells and Pomegranates series, were, for the most part, unsuccessful.

During this period Browning began to discover that his real talents lay in taking a single character and allowing that character to discover more about himself by revealing further personal aspects of himself in his speeches; the dramatic monologue. The techniques he developed through this—especially the use of diction, rhythm, and symbol—are regarded as his most important contribution to poetry. They would later influence such major poets of the 20th Century as Ezra Pound, T. S. Eliot, and Robert Frost.

By 1840, with the publication of Sordello, the tide turned somewhat. Many thought he was being deliberately obscure, opaque beyond measure and his poetry for the next decade or so was not eagerly acquired or talked about.

As Browning attempted to rehabilitate his career he began a relationship with Elizabeth Barrett in 1845. He had read her poems and, being totally charmed by their quality, was determined to meet her. The poetess was better known than the younger Browning but suffered from a debilitating illness and was also subject to the harsh behaviour of her over-bearing father. Nevertheless, the new couple were soon inseparable.

Her father, as he did with any of his children that married, disinherited her. Despite this she had some money from her own resources and sensing that the best outcome for both the relationship and her own health was to move abroad the couple did just that. After a private marriage at St Marylebone Parish Church, in September 1846, they journeyed to Europe to honeymoon in Paris.

Their new life now took them to Italy, first to Pisa and a little later to Florence. There they absorbed life and one another.

But in the short term the literary assault on Browning's work did not let up. He was now criticized by such patrician writers as Charles Kingsley for his abandonment of England for foreign lands. Browning could do little to answer these attacks except to compose with his pen and continue with his poetical journey.

The Browning's were well respected, and even famous. Elizabeth health began to improve, she grew stronger and in 1849, at the age of 43, between four miscarriages, she gave birth to a son, Robert Wiedeman Barrett Browning, whom they nicknamed "Penini" or "Pen",

Intriguingly despite his growing reputation and return to form as a poet he was more often than not known as 'Elizabeth Barrett's husband'.

Work flowed from his pen that was to ensure his reputation as one of England's leading poets. When his collection Men and Women was published in 1855 it contained some of his finest lines. It was dedicated to Elizabeth. Life had begun to smile handsome rewards upon the Brownings.

Victorian society was very much taken with all things spiritualist. It was not enough to have command of much of the globe through Empire, they wished to know and explore wherever they could. The spirit world beckoned their interest. Browning dissented from this view believing it was all a hoax and a fraud. Elizabeth, however, was inclined to believe and this caused several disagreements between the couple.

They attended a séance by Daniel Dunglas Home, in July 1855. (Home was a famous and clamored after Scottish physical medium with the reported ability to levitate and speak with the dead). It is said that during this séance a spirit face materialised. Home then claimed it was the face of Browning's son who had died in infancy. Browning seized the 'materialisation' which turned out to be Home's bare foot. Browning had never lost a son in infancy.

After the séance, Browning wrote an angry letter to The Times, in which he said: "the whole display of hands, spirit utterances etc., was a cheat and imposture."

The Browning's time in Italy were immensely rewarding years for both their personal and professional lives. Browning encouraged her to include Sonnets from the Portuguese in her published works, these beautiful poems are undoubtedly one of the highlights of English love poetry.

Elizabeth had become quite politicised during these years. Engrossed in Italian politics (which was continuing to slowly re-unify the country), she issued a small volume of political poems entitled Poems before Congress (1860) most of which were written to express her sympathy with the Italian cause after the earlier outbreak of The Second Italian Independence War in 1859. In England they caused uproar. Conservative magazines such as Blackwood's and the Saturday Review labelled her a fanatic. She dedicated the book to her husband.

But in 1861 tragedy struck.

The couple had spent the winter of 1860–61 in Rome when Elizabeth's health deteriorated again and they returned to Florence in early June. However, these turned out to be her final weeks. Only morphine would now still the pain. She died in Browning's arms on June 29th, 1861. Browning said that she died "smilingly, happily, and with a face like a girl's .... Her last word was .... "Beautiful".

Her burial took place in the nearby Protestant English Cemetery of Florence. The local people were deeply saddened, and shops closed their doors in grief and respect.

Browning and their son were obviously devastated. Unable to bear being in Florence without Elizabeth they soon returned to London to live at 19 Warwick Crescent, Maida Vale.

As he re-integrated himself back into the London literary scene he began to finally receive the proper praise, respect and reputation that his works deserved.

Browning went on to publish Dramatis Personæ (1864), and The Ring and the Book (1868–1869). The latter, based on an "old yellow book" which told of a seventeenth-century Italian murder trial, received wide and generous critical acclaim. Although by now he was in the twilight of a long and prolific career, that had achieved some notable ups and downs, he was respected and indeed renowned for his talents and works.

In 1878, he revisited Italy for the first time since Elizabeth's death. He would return there on several further occasions but never to Florence.

Such was the esteem he was held in that The Browning Society was founded in 1881. Although he had never obtained a degree (something that set him apart from many other Victorian poets) he was now awarded honorary degrees from Oxford University in 1882 and then the University of Edinburgh in 1884.

In 1887, Browning produced the major work of his later years, Parleyings with Certain People of Importance in Their Day. Browning now spoke with his own voice as he engaged in a series of dialogues with long-forgotten figures of literary, artistic, and philosophic history. Unfortunately, both the critics and public were completely baffled by this.

On April 7th, 1889 Browning attended a dinner party at the home of his friend, the artist Rudolf Lehmann. The highlight of which was a recording made on a wax cylinder on an Edison cylinder phonograph. On the recording, which still exists, Browning recites part of How They Brought the Good News from Ghent to Aix, and can even be heard apologising when he forgets the words.

The recording was first played in 1890 on the anniversary of his death, at a gathering of his admirers, it was said to be the first time anyone's voice 'had been heard from beyond the grave'.

His last work Asolando: Fancies and Facts (1889), returned to his brief and concise lyric verse that was so popular. It was published on the day of his death on December 12th, 1889, Robert Browning was at his son's home Ca' Rezzonico in Venice.

He was buried in Poets' Corner in Westminster Abbey; his grave lies immediately adjacent to that of Alfred Tennyson.

Among the many who have publicly acknowledged their literary debt to him are Henry James, Oscar Wilde, George Bernard Shaw, G. K. Chesterton, Ezra Pound, Jorge Luis Borges, and Vladimir Nabokov.

Robert Browning - A Concise Bibliography

Here follows a list of the plays and poetry volumes published during his lifetime. Poems of particular worth are noted from within those volumes.

Pauline: A Fragment of a Confession (1833)
Paracelsus (1835)
Strafford (play) (1837)
Sordello (1840)
Bells and Pomegranates No. I: Pippa Passes (play) (1841)
      The Year's at the Spring
Bells and Pomegranates No. II: King Victor and King Charles (play) (1842)
Bells and Pomegranates No. III: Dramatic Lyrics (1842)
      Porphyria's Lover
      Soliloquy of the Spanish Cloister
      My Last Duchess
      The Pied Piper of Hamelin
      Count Gismond
      Johannes Agricola in Meditation
Bells and Pomegranates No. IV: The Return of the Druses (play) (1843)
Bells and Pomegranates No. V: A Blot in the 'Scutcheon (play) (1843)
Bells and Pomegranates No. VI: Colombe's Birthday (play) (1844)
Bells and Pomegranates No. VII: Dramatic Romances and Lyrics (1845)
      The Laboratory
      How They Brought the Good News from Ghent to Aix
      The Bishop Orders His Tomb at Saint Praxed's Church
      The Lost Leader
      Home Thoughts from Abroad
      Meeting at Night
Bells and Pomegranates No. VIII: Luria and A Soul's Tragedy (plays) (1846)
Christmas-Eve and Easter-Day (1850)
An Essay on Percy Bysshe Shelley (essay) (1852)
Two Poems (1854)
Men and Women (1855)
      Love Among the Ruins
      A Toccata of Galuppi's
      Childe Roland to the Dark Tower Came
      Fra Lippo Lippi
      Andrea Del Sarto
      The Patriot
      The Last Ride Together
      Memorabilia
      Cleon

www.ingramcontent.com/pod-product-compliance
Lightning Source LLC
Chambersburg PA
CBHW060141050426
42448CB00010B/2233